D0386386

Making and Using the Atomic Bomb

Other books in the History Firsthand series:

Making and Using the Atomic Bomb

Mark McKain, *Book Editor*

Daniel Leone, *President*
Bonnie Szumski, *Publisher*
Scott Barbour, *Managing Editor*
David M. Haugen, *Series Editor*

GREENHAVEN
PRESS®

San Diego • Detroit • New York • San Francisco • Cleveland
New Haven, Conn. • Waterville, Maine • London • Munich

© 2003 by Greenhaven Press. Greenhaven Press is an imprint of The Gale Group, Inc., a division of Thomson Learning, Inc.

Greenhaven® and Thomson Learning™ are trademarks used herein under license.

For more information, contact
Greenhaven Press
27500 Drake Rd.
Farmington Hills, MI 48331-3535
Or you can visit our Internet site at http://www.gale.com

ALL RIGHTS RESERVED.
No part of this work covered by the copyright hereon may be reproduced or used in any form or by any means—graphic, electronic, or mechanical, including photocopying, recording, taping, Web distribution or information storage retrieval systems—without the written permission of the publisher.

Every effort has been made to trace the owners of copyrighted material.

Cover credit: © Hulton/Archive by Getty Images

LIBRARY OF CONGRESS CATALOGING-IN-PUBLICATION DATA

Making and using the atomic bomb / Mark McKain, book editor.
   p. cm. — (History firsthand)
Includes bibliographical references and index.
ISBN 0-7377-1413-1 (pbk. : alk. paper) — ISBN 0-7377-1412-3 (lib. : alk. paper)
   1. Atomic bomb—United States—History—20th century. 2. Manhattan Project
(U.S.) I. McKain, Mark. II. Series.
QC773.3.U5 M23 2003
355.8'25119'0973—dc21
                                    2002027880

Contents

Chapter 1: Discovery of Fission

1. Energy from Nuclei
by Otto R. Frisch   39
In December 1938, Otto R. Frisch visited his aunt,
Lise Meitner, in Sweden. The two made some calculations on scraps of paper while taking a walk in the
snow. These preliminary equations suggested that the
splitting of an atomic nucleus should give off tremendous energy. After working out some of the theoretical details, Frisch dubbed the intriguing process
"nuclear fission."

2. Publishing the Secret of Fission
by Leo Szilard   48
Working in America in 1939, Leo Szilard, Enrico
Fermi, and others confirmed, "the large scale liberation of atomic energy was just around the corner."
These scientists had not performed any practical experiments, but they recognized that a powerful explosive device could be based on the chain reaction
caused by splitting a uranium atom. Since war was
just starting in Europe, the scientists had to decide
whether to keep their findings secret or publish them
and tell the world.

3. Warning of the Dangers of Nuclear Technology
by Edward Teller   56
Once the secret of nuclear fission was revealed, members of the American team of scientists working on
atomic research believed the government should be
warned of the potential threat that nuclear technology
posed to the safety of the country and the world. Leo
Szilard and Edward Teller enlisted the aid of Albert
Einstein in drafting a letter to President Franklin D.

Roosevelt to advise him that other governments—
including that of Nazi Germany—had scientists
working on nuclear fission and could develop
weapons that would endanger the security of the
United States.

Chapter 2: The Manhattan Project

and plutonium, the two elements used in the explosive devices aboard America's first two atomic bombs.

Chapter 3: Using the Bomb

using the atomic bomb against Japan. Instead the Franck report argued that a demonstration of the weapon on an unpopulated island would be enough to convince the Japanese to surrender. The scientists also predicted that using the weapon would promote a nuclear arms race that would eventually threaten the safety of the United States.

using atomic weapons against an enemy. Truman outlines all the factors that went into making the fateful decision as well as the attempts that were made to force Japan to surrender beforehand. Ultimately, Truman insists that his decision was the correct one and that it shortened the war and saved hundreds of thousands of lives.

Chapter 4: The Aftermath

4. The Need for a National Nuclear Energy Program
by the Atomic Energy Commission
The Atomic Energy Commission was the civilian
successor to the military Manhattan Project. Its chief
responsibility was to find peaceful uses for atomic
energy. In 1962, the commission informed President
John F. Kennedy that nuclear power could supply
America with a cheap energy source. In its report to
the president, the commission advocated a national
program of building nuclear reactors to provide for
the nation's electrical and power needs.

Foreword

In his preface to a book on the events leading to the Civil War, Stephen B. Oates, the historian and biographer of Abraham Lincoln, John Brown, and other noteworthy American historical figures, explained the difficulty of writing history in the traditional third-person voice of the biographer and historian. "The trouble, I realized, was the detached third-person voice," wrote Oates. "It seemed to wring all the life out of my characters and the antebellum era." Indeed, how can a historian, even one as prominent as Oates, compete with the eloquent voices of Daniel Webster, Abraham Lincoln, Harriet Beecher Stowe, Frederick Douglass, and Robert E. Lee?

Oates's comment notwithstanding, every student of history, professional and amateur alike, can name a score of excellent accounts written in the traditional third-person voice of the historian that bring to life an event or an era and the people who lived through it. In *Battle Cry of Freedom*, James M. McPherson vividly re-creates the American Civil War. Barbara Tuchman's *The Guns of August* captures in sharp detail the tensions in Europe that led to the outbreak of World War I. Taylor Branch's *Parting the Waters* provides a detailed and dramatic account of the American Civil Rights Movement. The study of history would be impossible without such guiding texts.

Nonetheless, Oates's comment makes a compelling point. Often the most convincing tellers of history are those who lived through the event, the eyewitnesses who recorded their firsthand experiences in autobiographies, speeches, memoirs, journals, and letters. The Greenhaven Press History Firsthand series presents history through the words of first-person narrators. Each text in this series captures a significant historical era or event—the American Civil War, the

Great Depression, the Holocaust, the Roaring Twenties, the 1960s, the Vietnam War. Readers will investigate these historical eras and events by examining primary-source documents, authored by chroniclers both famous and little known. The texts in the History Firsthand series comprise the celebrated and familiar words of the presidents, generals, and famous men and women of letters who recorded their impressions for posterity, as well as the statements of the ordinary people who struggled to understand the storm of events around them—the foot soldiers who fought the great battles and their loved ones back home, the men and women who waited on the breadlines, the college students who marched in protest.

The texts in this series are particularly suited to students beginning serious historical study. By examining these firsthand documents, novice historians can begin to form their own insights and conclusions about the historical era or event under investigation. To aid the student in that process, the texts in the History Firsthand series include introductions that provide an overview of the era or event, timelines, and bibliographies that point the serious student toward key historical works for further study.

The study of history commences with an examination of words—the testimony of witnesses who lived through an era or event and left for future generations the task of making sense of their accounts. The Greenhaven Press History Firsthand series invites the beginner historian to commence the process of historical investigation by focusing on the words of those individuals who made history by living through it and recording their experiences firsthand.

Introduction: History of the Atomic Bomb

A brilliant flash brighter than the light of several suns lit up the dawn. A deafening crack thundered against the nearby mountains. A huge fireball rose above the desert floor and transformed itself into a towering mushroom cloud thirty-eight thousand feet tall. Military officers and scientists stood watching in shock and awe. The cataclysmic sight of the first test explosion of the atomic bomb reminded scientist J. Robert Oppenheimer of the words of Shiva in the sacred Hindu text, the *Bhagavad-Gita:* "I am become death, the destroyer of worlds."[1]

This blinding flash of light at Alamogordo, New Mexico, heralded the dawn of the atomic age on July 16, 1945. Less than a month later the Japanese cities of Hiroshima and Nagasaki would be devastated by the atomic bomb's destructive power. Soon after, Japan would surrender and World War II would be over. But the threat of future devastation did not end with the war. In 1949, the United States would lose its monopoly on atomic weapons when Russia exploded its own nuclear device. The two superpowers squared off and the ensuing arms race ushered in the Cold War. Eventually other nations acquired "the bomb," and the potential for nuclear annihilation still haunts the world. But along with the shadow of destruction came the harnessing of nuclear energy, a cheap and efficient source of energy with great promise. It is undeniable that these two aspects of nuclear technology have greatly impacted life on the planet. And the seeds of this great discovery began with a few key experiments in the first part of the twentieth century.

Early Discoveries

In the early decades of the twentieth century, scientists were uncovering the structure of the atom. They discovered the existence of negatively charged particles, electrons, orbiting positively charged protons in the nucleus—the center—of an atom. In 1932, two British physicists, Ernest Rutherford and James Chadwick predicted and found the neutron—the last puzzle piece in the atomic structure. The neutron, along with a number of protons, formed the nucleus of an atom. The neutron turned out to be the key particle that would unlock the secret of atomic energy.

Because the neutron was electrically neutral and would not be deflected by the charged particles in the atom, scientists could use neutrons to bombard the nucleus of atoms and further explore their structure. Enrico Fermi, an Italian physicist, began bombarding elements with neutrons just after Rutherford and Chadwick's discovery in 1934. Fermi used radon, a radioactive gas derived from radium, as his neutron source. Fermi's radon could emit 1 million neutrons per second. When he aimed the radon-produced neutrons at uranium, a strange reaction took place and radioactivity was produced. Fermi did not completely understand what was going on in his experiments. According to Edward Teller, one of Fermi's fellow physicists, Fermi barely missed discovering the splitting of the atom because of his careful laboratory procedures:

> Fermi was a very careful experimenter. He covered his uranium with a thin sheet of inert material to stop the normal alpha particles [helium atoms emitted in the reaction] . . . in which he was not interested. That sheet also stopped the fission products, which had a short range but extremely high energy-density. Had Fermi forgotten to cover his sample even once, fission would have been discovered years earlier.[2]

After a chemical analysis of his irradiated uranium, Fermi tentatively concluded that the uranium had been changed into an unknown element heavier than uranium. This turned out not to be the case, as Fermi was later to learn, but he published his results in a leading scientific magazine so that other scientists might improve on his experiment.

The Discovery of Fission

Another group of scientists in Berlin, Germany, decided to repeat Fermi's experiments in 1938. Otto Hahn and Fritz Strassmann bombarded uranium with neutrons. When they analyzed the results of the subsequent reaction, they found they had produced barium atoms. Hahn and Strassmann were two of the very best chemists in Europe. Their chemical analysis of the uranium reaction was much more exhaustive than Fermi's, and yet they could hardly believe what they were finding. It was almost unthinkable that barium, an element almost half as heavy as uranium, would be produced by a neutron absorbed into the uranium nucleus. This result was puzzling because it was not known at the time that atoms could split and transform into other types of elements. Hahn and Strassmann also discovered that their original sample of uranium had lost a small amount of weight. Like Fermi, Hahn and Strassmann could not explain their results.

During the time Hahn and Strassmann were doing their experiments, the German dictator Adolf Hitler initiated his plan to eliminate, or expel, the Jews of Germany. Hitler's Nazi Party tormented Jews, destroyed their homes and businesses, and made many arrests. In a few short days in early November 1938 the Nazis imprisoned thirty-five thousand Jews and transported them to concentration camps. It was the beginning of Hitler's "final solution"—the genocide of European Jewry.

Hahn and Strassmann sent a letter to their colleague, Lise Meitner, who until recently had worked with them in Berlin. Meitner was a Jewish physicist from Austria. She had kept her position as a physicist in Germany because of her Austrian citizenship. When Hitler's troops invaded Austria, she became a German subject and was forced to flee to Denmark. There she joined her physicist nephew, Otto Frisch, who was working with another world famous scientist, Niels Bohr, on the forces in the atom. In the letter to Meitner, Hahn told her of the puzzling results of their experiment with uranium, and asked her help in interpreting what was occurring in the reaction.

Meitner was spending the Christmas holidays in Sweden and invited Frisch to join her. One evening, on a walk through the snow, they tackled the questions posed by Hahn and Strassmann's experiment. After working for over three hours in the cold, their calculations finally gave them the answer. They determined that the uranium atom had been stretched like a drop of water until it split in two. This split produced the lighter barium atoms. They also calculated that the missing weight had transformed into energy, the radioactivity that Fermi had recorded earlier. On their walk in the snow, Meitner and Frisch had solved what Fermi, Hahn, and Strassmann could not. More significantly, Meitner and Frisch determined that the energy produced in the splitting of one uranium atom was approximately 200 million electron volts. This was a huge amount of energy for such a small reaction. Later, Frisch would give a name to this specific process of releasing energy from an atom: He called it "fission."

European Scientists Flee to America

As the secrets of atomic energy were being revealed in Europe in 1938 and 1939, Hitler was invading Czechoslovakia and Poland, sparking off the Second World War. The Nazis stepped up their persecution of the Jews. Jewish scientists were condemned for their race and for their "Jewish physics," which the Nazis claimed were diseased and corrupt. The Nazis' anti-Semitism caused many leading scientists, including Max Born, James Franck, Edward Teller, Leo Szilard, and Eugene Wigner, to flee to America where they all would play an instrumental role in the development of the atomic bomb. One top physicist who did not flee from the Nazis was Werner Heisenberg. In deciding to stay in Germany, Heisenberg became a tool of the Nazis and eventually headed the German effort to build atomic weapons.

Enrico Fermi was another European scientist who was affected by Hitler's anti-Semitic policies. Fermi, an Italian physicist, was not Jewish, but his wife, Laura, was. When Italy became allied with Germany, Fermi knew his wife was in danger. In 1938, Fermi was awarded the Nobel Prize for physics. When he traveled to Sweden to receive the prize, he used the opportunity to emigrate to America, where he had secretly secured a teaching job at Columbia University in New York City.

In 1939, Niels Bohr temporarily joined the ranks of the émigrés. Earlier, in 1938, Bohr gave a speech condemning Nazi racism at an international scientific conference in Denmark. The German delegation of scientists walked out in protest. Bohr believed passionately that the purpose of science was "the gradual removal of prejudices."[3] Bohr traveled to the United States to attend a conference of theoretical physics at George Washington University in Washington, D.C. Before the conference had begun, George Gamow, the organizer of the conference, had called Edward Teller, exclaiming, "Bohr has gone crazy. He says uranium splits."[4] At the conference, Bohr spread the news of the splitting of the atom by Hahn and Strassmann as well as the calculations done by Frisch and Meitner. Scientists in America, including Fermi and Szilard, literally ran to their labs to duplicate and check the experiment that had split the uranium atom.

After the conference, Bohr stayed at Princeton to work on fission. Bohr had concluded that nuclear energy was a practical reality. But he saw that

> The loop needed for a chain reaction is this: Fissions produce neutrons, and neutrons produce fissions. . . . But because the rate of fission he saw was a hundred times lower than expected, Bohr guessed that only the rare isotope U-235 was involved. He concluded that the chain reaction would not work in natural uranium (which is almost pure U-238). Separating out the tiny fraction of U-235 would be incredibly difficult because isotopes have similar properties.[5]

Isotopes are atoms of the same element, but they have different atomic weights. For example, a uranium atom can have an extra neutron and still have the same properties as the uranium atom without the extra neutron. However, the extra neutron in the uranium nucleus makes the nucleus unbalanced or unstable. The extra neutron will spontaneously change to a proton and in the process emit a high-speed electron. This electron is a form of energy called radiation. The unbalance caused by the extra neutron causes the uranium atom to split, releasing energy and more neutrons to be emitted, and initiating the chain reaction loop.

Einstein's Letter to Roosevelt

In 1939, as the Nazis seemed intent on invading all of Europe, Enrico Fermi, Leo Szilard, and Edward Teller were among those who saw the destructive potential of a nuclear reaction. They realized that if a self-sustaining chain reaction were possible, this chain reaction would take place in an instant, releasing a huge amount of energy culminating in a tremendous explosion if uncontrolled. On the other hand, if the reaction could be controlled, the energy produced could drive generators that made electricity. Such controlled nuclear power could be a cheap and plentiful source of energy for all humankind.

Despite the great promise of atomic energy, the image that haunted the scientists was that of Hitler possessing an atomic bomb. This vision was especially frightening to Leo Szilard and Eugene Wigner, who had experienced firsthand the terrors of the Nazis when they invaded Szilard's and Wigner's native country, Hungary. The pair decided that the American authorities must be informed. They drafted a letter to President Roosevelt warning him that atomic energy could be used to develop a powerful weapon and that Germany would certainly try to build one. The letter did not specifically advise the United States to develop an atom bomb, but did urge the president to "secure a supply of uranium ore for the United States" and "to speed up the experimental work" on nuclear research "by providing funds."[6] They brought their letter to Albert Einstein to sign because they thought his great reputation would help get the president's attention. Einstein had come to the United States in 1933. He was one of the first prominent European scientists who had been expelled from Germany for no other reason than being Jewish. Although Einstein was an avowed pacifist he signed the letter stating, "the element uranium may be turned into a new and important source of energy . . . extremely powerful bombs of a new type may thus be constructed."[7] They then gave the letter to Alexander Sachs, an influential friend of President Roosevelt. Einstein's letter had the effect Szilard, Wigner, Fermi, and Teller had hoped for. Roosevelt funded the Advisory Committee on Uranium to find out if atomic weapons could actually be produced.

At the same time in Great Britain, Otto Frisch and another immigrant German scientist, Rudolph Peierls, wrote a secret report on nuclear fission for the British government. Their report stated that to make a nuclear reaction turn critical and produce a devastating explosion one pound of uranium would be needed. A subsequent report by the MAUD Committee (a group of British government officials and scientists who were given the code name MAUD) used the Frisch-Peierls memorandum as the basis of their findings. The MAUD report concluded that with present technology and supplies of fissionable uranium, any scientifically advanced nation could manufacture an atomic bomb before the end of the war. The British government shared its findings with the United States. President Roosevelt received a copy of the MAUD report just before the Japanese attacked Pearl Harbor on December 7, 1941. Shortly thereafter, Roosevelt decided to commit the nation to building an atomic bomb before Germany could create one.

Creation of the Manhattan Project

Roosevelt placed the responsibility of building the bomb with the U.S. Army Corps of Engineers. The Corps of Engineers supervises the army's engineering projects. A separate district manages each project. Colonel J.C. Marshall was ordered to set up a new and extremely secret district to develop the atomic bomb. Because Marshall's office was in New York City, this new district was called the Manhattan Engineer District, and his top-secret mission was code-named the Manhattan Project. At first, the Manhattan Project was beset with organizational problems. Many scientists did not want to work directly for the military. More tensions surfaced when Colonel Marshall selected Stone & Webster, a Boston engineering firm, to supervise the construction of uranium production plants. Many scientists objected to this arrangement. As Glen Seaborg, codiscoverer of plutonium, wrote: "A number of the people present expressed great concern about working for an industrial contractor because of their fear this would not be a compatible environment."[8] These and other problems hampered the Manhattan Project during its first months of operation in the summer of 1942. It would take the appointment of Brigadier General Leslie Richard Groves as the new military head of the Manhattan Project in September 1942 to work out these problems and get things moving.

The First Atomic Pile

Some of the early work on the development of the bomb took place at the University of Chicago. The lab in Chicago was called the Metallurgical Laboratory (or Met Lab). Metallurgical means the study of metals, but the name was used only as a cover for its real work on the Manhattan Project. One of the first tasks the Met Lab was given was to ascertain whether a nuclear chain reaction could sustain itself in order to reach the critical stage and produce an explosion. As yet, the potential destructive power of a chain reaction was purely theoretical. If a bomb were to be created, the scientists would need to know that uranium could reliably sustain a chain reaction.

Enrico Fermi and Leo Szilard were at the center of this work. They orchestrated the construction of an atomic pile—a crude atomic reactor—in a squash court beneath an abandoned stadium on the south side of Chicago. Fermi's wife, Laura, related that "Szilard and Fermi conceived a contrivance that they thought might produce a chain reaction. It would be made of uranium and very pure graphite disposed in layers: layers exclusively of graphite would alternate with layers in which uranium chunks would be imbedded in graphite. In other words, it would be a 'pile.'"[9]

It took six weeks of labor to stack the layers of uranium and graphite to form a large sphere. The graphite served as a moderator to slow down the bombarding neutrons so that they could be absorbed by the uranium atoms, splitting them and emitting more neutrons to continue the chain reaction. On December 2, 1942, the pile was ready for its crucial test. Fermi ordered his technicians to begin retracting cadmium control rods from the pile. As long as the rods were stuck in the pile, the cadmium metal absorbed neutrons and prevented the uranium from reacting. As the rods were withdrawn, radioactive counters clicked, indicating the nuclear reaction had begun. Fermi proceeded slowly, making calculations and predicting various stages of the reaction. There were dangers: The pile could overheat and burst into flames, or an explosion with a release of radiation could occur. These dangers were supposed to be unlikely, but no one knew what might happen. By 3:20 P.M. the instruments showed a continuous rise in the production of neutrons. "The reaction is self-sustaining,"[10] Fermi said matter-of-factly, and the rods were reinserted into the pile, shutting down the reaction. The first atomic chain reaction had been achieved.

Manufacturing Fuel for the Bomb

Before assuming command of the Manhattan Project, Brigadier General Leslie R. Groves had directed the construction of the Pentagon, the huge office complex that housed the Department of Defense. Groves at first balked at the assignment to take charge of the Manhattan Project because he wanted a combat command. But when he realized that the atomic bomb could win the war for the United States, he enthusiastically brought his considerable energies and management skills to the project.

Within days of his appointment, Groves began in earnest.

First, he needed a manufacturing site for separating uranium. As Niels Bohr had discovered in 1939, to make the bomb, a rare form of uranium—U-235—was needed. This isotope of uranium is much more efficient in reacting with neutrons and producing a fission reaction than U-238, the common isotope found in nature. U-235 appears only in extremely small amounts within uranium ore. To obtain it, U-235 must be separated out of the bulk ore. At the time, scientists were still working on various methods to separate and refine uranium. These methods included high-speed centrifuges, gaseous diffusion, liquid thermal diffusion, and electromagnetic separation. Despite the fact that none of these costly and time-consuming methods had proved reliable, Groves knew that he would need a large industrial site to house the equipment necessary for the process. The refining site needed to be away from large populations, in an area where secrecy and security could be maintained. After considering several sites, Groves chose Oak Ridge, Tennessee, to refine the U-235 fuel for the first atomic bomb.

Meanwhile, a group of physicists, including Ernest Lawrence, Edwin McMillan, Glenn Seaborg, Joseph Kennedy, and Arthur Wahl, discovered the new element of plutonium. Plutonium is even more efficient than uranium at producing a fission reaction. It is also easier to manufacture because it is the by-product of the nuclear reaction in an atomic pile. When Groves learned of the new material, he established a separate manufacturing site at Hanford, Washington, to produce plutonium. The plutonium fuel for the second bomb—the one dropped on Nagasaki, Japan—was manufactured at the Hanford site.

Groves's experience in managing large industrial projects served him well in constructing these vital manufacturing complexes. Despite objections by many scientists in the Manhattan Project, Groves insisted that a commercial engineering company help design, construct, and run the Oakridge and Hanford refineries. Groves wanted the DuPont company to do this because of its experience in chemical manufacturing. DuPont was very hesitant to get involved in the strange top-secret project. Groves finally persuaded DuPont executives to construct and furnish the two complexes. With the company's engineers on board, the scientists could begin production. Scientists estimated that about ten pounds of fissionable material would be needed for the first few bombs, but it would take some time for the two plants working together to manufacture even this small amount.

Establishing the Los Alamos Laboratory

After overseeing the construction of the uranium and plutonium plants, Groves moved on to the actual construction of the bomb. In October 1942, he selected J. Robert Oppenheimer to direct the scientific research and design of the bomb. Oppenheimer had attended Harvard University during the 1920s. He had also studied physics with Chadwick and Rutherford in Great Britain. He earned his doctorate in Germany where he gained an international reputation as a physicist. When Oppenheimer returned to the United States, he got a job at the University of California. There he became a leader in atomic research. It was while he was working in California that he was chosen by Groves to direct the scientific effort of the Manhattan Project.

Oppenheimer and Groves were in agreement that the Manhattan Project needed a central laboratory where scientists could collaborate on theoretical problems as well as the physical construction of the bomb. On December 7, 1942, Groves selected Los Alamos, an isolated town in the mountains of New Mexico that provided both secrecy and security. The specific site chosen had formerly been a private boys' school, but under the army's supervision, it quickly grew into a large complex with laboratories, housing, and all the support facilities needed by a small community. At the end of the war, sixty-five hundred people were working at Los Alamos including physicists, chemists, metallurgists, technicians, construction workers, clerical staff, and their families. With the establishment of Los Alamos as the weapons laboratory, and the construction of the uranium and plutonium factories at Oakridge and Hanford, the actual work of making a bomb could now begin.

Oppenheimer recruited the finest physicists in the country to develop the bomb. Some were attracted by the call to patriotism; others were drawn by the new and challenging work. In addition to American scientists, many of whom were European immigrants, a contingent of British scientists worked at Los Alamos: Niels Bohr, Otto Frisch, Hans Bethe, Rudolf Peierls, and Klaus Fuchs, among others. One of these British scientists, Fuchs, was on a secret mission unknown to either government. Fuchs had immigrated to England from Nazi Germany in 1933. He had a solid reputation as a physicist, but, as was later learned, during his entire time at Los Alamos, Fuchs was passing information about the atomic bomb to the Russians.

Little Boy and Fat Man

As the Los Alamos scientists approached the design of the uranium-based bomb, one of their main problems was how to prevent it from exploding prematurely. It takes only a small amount of uranium, about the size of a baseball, to produce a critical mass resulting in a tremendous nuclear explosion. The problem was how to bring together the critical mass at the right moment. The scientists solved this problem by using a gun barrel inside the bomb to fire a bullet of subcritical uranium at a target of subcritical uranium. The rapid impact of the two masses would make a critical mass large enough to produce a chain reaction and a nuclear explosion. The resulting bomb that used this bullet method was called "Little Boy" because its internal gun barrel made it long and thin. The gun barrel design was simple and reliable. Oppenheimer and the scientists at Los Alamos were very confident of its design and did not feel they needed a test to prove it worked.

While the gun barrel was a practical design solution for the uranium bomb, it would not work for the plutonium bomb. Plutonium fissions more easily than uranium and the scientists needed a faster way of bringing the two subcritical masses of plutonium together or else a partial reaction might occur before all the material interacted. Physicist Seth Neddermeyer and mathematician John von Neumann proposed a design in which a ring of conventional explosives surrounded a small sphere of plutonium. When the explosives were detonated, they formed a lens that focused the blast energy toward the single plutonium sphere, compressing it into a dense supercritical mass. The implosion design eliminated the need for two masses of plutonium. The bomb that housed this triggering device was circular in shape, measuring five feet in diameter and nine feet in length. It looked like a large egg and was given the name "Fat Man." Its innovative implosion design worked on paper, but Oppenheimer was skeptical of it functioning properly. He decided that it would have to be tested before he could be sure it would work on the battlefield.

The Trinity Test

Brigadier General Groves was at first opposed to the test firing. He was afraid that the huge explosion would jeopardize the secrecy of the bomb and use up scarce plutonium. Oppenheimer finally persuaded him that a test was necessary. The test site, the army's Alamogordo bombing range in New Mexico, was selected for its desolate isolation. It was miles from any town, thus minimizing the danger that radioactive fallout would reach civilian areas. Oppenheimer codenamed the site "Trinity" after a line from a poem by John Dunne. He stipulated that a tower be erected to cradle the plutonium bomb. After months of construction, the area designated as ground zero was complete. The desert floor was strewn with miles of wires that ran from the tower to the command center ten thousand yards away. These controlled the detonation of the bomb as well as instruments to measure its effects.

The fateful moment came on July 16, 1945. Important scientists and top military generals came from across the country to witness the test. Tensions ran high as the last piece of plutonium was inserted, and the large Fat Man bomb was hauled to the top of the one-hundred-foot tower.

The test was delayed by rain for several hours, but when the storm cleared, Groves set the new detonation time for 5:30 A.M. At 5:29 A.M. a flash of light lit up the dawn with a brilliance many times that of the sun. A tremendous roar echoed against the surrounding desert mountains. People in the towns as far away as Santa Fe and El Paso saw the fireball shooting six miles in the air. Windows were blown out in Gallup, New Mexico, 235 miles away. The test of the plutonium bomb was a complete success. The explosion was even stronger than most had predicted. It had vaporized the tower and blown a twelve-hundred-foot crater in the desert floor, fusing sand into green glass. Plant and animal life had also been incinerated, leaving only blackened shadows burned into the rocks and dirt. These were the birth signs of a new age—the atomic age.

The German Atomic Bomb

By the time the Trinity Test was completed at Los Alamos, the American, British, and Canadian armies had successfully launched the D-Day invasion on the beaches of Normandy, France. The tide of war had changed. Within months, the American forces had liberated Paris and pushed the German army back to its own borders. With Russian armies pushing in from the east and the Americans and British crossing the Rhine into Germany proper, the Nazi dream was all but dead. On April 30, Hitler took his own life, and seven days later Germany surrendered.

Even before the end, as the Allied armies rolled into Germany, they discovered the horror of the concentration camps where millions of Jews had been put to death. The American army also discovered scientific laboratories with documents on the German effort to develop an atomic bomb. A special unit of scientists and intelligence officers known as Alsos investigated the German program. They found the German atomic pile in a cave in the Black Forest as well as a cache of uranium ore. They captured German scientists and spirited them away to Britain. After two years, the Alsos investigation determined that while the Germans were engaged in atomic bomb research, Hitler had never fully supported the program, and as a result, it was largely ineffective. The German scientists had not even produced a successful chain reaction. Nazi Germany, in purging itself of its top physicists, most of whom were Jewish, had given the nuclear advantage to the Americans. But the American atomic bomb was developed too late to be used to win the war in Europe. It was not too late, however, for the atomic bomb to be used in the Pacific war against the Japanese.

The Bomb Is Readied

With Germany out of the war, the Americans hoped Japan would surrender. Japan, however, remained defiant. Harry S. Truman—who took over as president on April 12, 1945, upon the sudden death of Franklin D. Roosevelt—ordered Brigadier General Groves to have the bomb ready to help win the war against Japan. In July 1945, Groves sent the plutonium and uranium bomb components to Tinian Island, a small island airbase in the Pacific. Navy captain William Parsons, an explosives expert, received the bomb at Tinian. He had worked with the bomb at Los Alamos and was in charge of assembling and arming both bombs. The Fat Man bomb, for instance, had to be put together from the separately shipped parts, including the plutonium core, high explosive lenses, electrical firing unit, and the detonators. The uranium Little Boy bomb was less complicated. By August both Fat Man and Little Boy bombs were ready for use.

Even though the new weapons stood ready, the decision to use them had not been made. Though he had served as vice president under Roosevelt, Truman had no previous knowledge of the atomic bomb until he became commander in chief. He quickly learned that the nuclear devices could possibly destroy an entire city. The decision to employ such weapons would not be made easily.

As the Trinity Test was being conducted, President Truman was in Potsdam, Germany, meeting with British prime minister Winston Churchill, and Russian premier Joseph Stalin. These three leaders of the Allied powers were meeting to negotiate the terms of the peace treaty with Germany. Truman had received a coded message on July 17, 1945, stating that the Trinity Test had been a complete success. He was delighted with the news. America now assuredly possessed a method that could bring about a quick end to the war. When he told Stalin that America had developed a powerful new weapon, Stalin's only comment was that he hoped Truman would use it against Japan. Despite the fact that America and Russia were allies in the war, Truman did not trust Stalin enough to divulge the details of the atomic bomb. But in fact, due to the espionage activities of Klaus Fuchs at Los Alamos, Stalin may have known all about the new weapon. Truman, however, did know that Russian armies had been searching their part of eastern Germany looking for stray German scientists and documents relating to the Nazi efforts in nuclear research. He was not about to help them further by relating American and British discoveries.

The Russians had a secret agreement with the other Allies to declare war against Japan in August, well after American forces had pushed Japanese armies back to their home islands. Truman did not relish Soviet aid in the Pacific war. He knew that Stalin would demand part of any conquered territory in the Pacific, and the Americans wanted to keep the Russians out of the region. Now with the atomic bomb at its disposal, the United States would not need Russia to defeat the Japanese.

To Use or Not to Use the Bomb

As Truman hurried back to the United States from Potsdam, he faced the final decision of whether to utilize the new atomic weapons. Truman had several committees of experts that were advising him on the matter. One such committee was the Interim Committee. This committee was composed of top scientists, and military and government officials including Secretary of War Henry Stimson, General George C. Marshall, Enrico Fermi, and J. Robert Oppenheimer. The committee unanimously recommended that the atomic bomb be used against Japan as soon as possible and without warning. The only other choice was to stage an invasion of the Japanese islands, and the cost in lives for both sides was too staggering—even compared to the losses expected from an atomic blast.

Not all scientists and political advisors, however, were in favor of using the bomb against Japan. Physicist Leo Szilard, the man who in 1939 had composed the letter to Roosevelt, was now gathering signatures to urge President Truman not to use the new weapon. What Szilard feared most was that dropping the bomb would eventually lead to an uncontrollable arms race that would put the world in jeopardy of nuclear devastation. Although Szilard gathered many signatures from important scientists in the Manhattan Project, his letter was intercepted by the military before it reached the president.

In addition to Szilard's outspoken opposition, Admiral William D. Leahy, a trusted and close advisor to the president, was concerned with the appalling destructiveness of the bomb. He labeled it an immoral and barbarous weapon akin to gas and germ warfare. Secretary Stimson also advised Truman to use the bomb only against military targets and not against innocent civilian populations. One alternative, proposed by physicist James Franck in a report to Secretary Stimson, was a demonstration of an atomic explosion on an uninhabited island with a representative from the Japanese government present. This proposed demonstration, it was hoped, would show the Japanese they could not win the war against such an overwhelming weapon.

Truman's Decision

The decision to use the atomic bomb could not be made by committee. Only one man, President Truman, could ultimately make the decision. Truman knew that his was a grave and awesome responsibility. At the Potsdam Conference he issued an ultimatum that demanded Japan surrender or face total destruction. The ultimatum did not reveal the true nature of the nuclear weapons possessed by the United States. The Potsdam ultimatum was the last hope of avoiding the use of the atomic bomb.

American military commanders were planning to invade the southern Japanese island of Kyushu on November 1, 1945. Estimates for the loss of American life in these battles ranged from 250,000 to 500,000 and higher. The Japanese casualties were expected to be much higher. Those in favor of using the bomb hoped that the destruction of cities in the Japanese homeland would provide a shocking psychological blow to the nation's leaders, convincing them they could not win against an enemy who possessed such a weapon. In the end, Truman agreed that the awesome new weapon could save hundreds of thousands of American and Japanese lives.

When the Japanese refused the Potsdam ultimatum to surrender, Truman signed the order to drop the bomb on Hiroshima, Japan. Hiroshima was chosen out of four cities recommended as prime targets. It ranked first on the list because it was an important city to the Japanese war effort. Its factories produced military equipment for the Japanese army, and over forty-three thousand troops were stationed at Hiroshima. Its port was a critical naval base, and it would be from this military complex that the Japanese generals would command the defense of southern Japan against the coming American invasion. However, in this important military city, there also lived 280,000 innocent civilians.

Flight over Hiroshima

General Carl Spaatz, the commander of the 509th Composite Group, a squadron of B-29 bombers modified to drop the bomb, received orders to bomb Hiroshima any time after August 3. His orders now included the city of Nagasaki as one of the possible alternate targets should Hiroshima prove unfeasible. The weather over Hiroshima kept the planes grounded until August 6. At 2:45 A.M., Lieutenant Colonel Paul W. Tibbets took off from Tinian Island in the *Enola Gay*, a plane he named after his mother. He was carrying the Little Boy bomb. To prevent Tinian from being blown up if the plane crashed on takeoff, William Parsons was to finish arming the bomb on the way to Hiroshima. Two observer planes accompanied the *Enola Gay* to record the explosion. At 7:30 Parsons completed arming the bomb and Tibbets brought the plane up to 31,000 feet. The *Enola Gay* had to be over eight miles away from ground zero if they were to survive the blast. At 9:15 the bombardier, Thomas Ferebee, released the bomb. Forty-three seconds later, Little Boy exploded 1,900 feet above Hiroshima with the force of 12,500 tons of TNT.

Witnesses on the ground said they saw a flash of light, instantly followed by a wave of heat so intense that it melted skin from bodies. Everything within a mile of ground zero was annihilated. Almost everyone in this radius was killed instantly. Houses three miles from the center were flattened. Thousands of people were hit by flying debris and trapped in collapsing buildings. Fires broke out all over the city ignited by the over 3,000-degree-Fahrenheit fireball of the bomb. Many thousands more died in the flames. A "black rain" fell, composed of radioactive fallout and ash. Some people died from this immediately while others took from one to five years to die from radioactive poisoning. At least 70,000 were killed that day. By the end of the year over half the population had died, approximately 140,000. Ninety percent of the city's buildings were destroyed including city offices, hospitals, fire departments, railroads, post offices, and radio and television stations. The entire municipal support system had been destroyed. For the thousands of wounded survivors there was little that could be done for their injuries.

Nagasaki

Only hours after Little Boy was dropped, President Truman released a public statement informing the world of the destruction of Hiroshima by the atomic bomb. Truman further pledged to continue bombing Japan with the new weapon if they did not surrender. The Japanese leaders at first thought Truman was only making threats. Because all communications with Hiroshima had been cut off, they had not yet received news of what had happened to the city. When they did learn of the utter destruction of Hiroshima, the Japanese leadership decided to continue fighting. On August 8, 1945, the Soviet Union declared war on Japan and began pushing the Japanese forces out of Manchuria.

Three days after Hiroshima, a B-29 bomber took off from Tinian. It was carrying the ten-thousand-pound Fat Man plutonium bomb that was identical to the one that had exploded in the Trinity Test. Captain Frederick C. Bock piloted the plane toward the primary target of Kokura. But as they got closer, the city was shrouded in fog. Bock and his crew proceeded to the secondary target, Nagasaki, which also turned out to be cloudy. The mission was almost scrubbed, but at the last minute there was a break in the clouds and Fat Man was dropped.

The blast from the Fat Man bomb was equal to twenty-two thousand tons of TNT—almost twice that of the Hiroshima blast. The explosion killed forty thousand people instantly. The fireball and black rain of radiation killed many thousands more. Nagasaki's buildings and infrastructure were destroyed, leaving treatment for the survivors virtually nonexistent. As happened at Hiroshima, half of the city's population, at least one hundred thousand, would die as a result of the effects of the bomb. A third bomb was being readied for use but it would never be dropped. The next day, on August 10, the Japanese surrendered. From August 6 to August 9—less than one week's time—150,000 people died in Japan as the result of the two atomic bombs.

The surrender of Japan ended World War II. It was the bloodiest war ever fought. Seventeen million soldiers lost their lives in the conflict. The civilian loss was even more horrific. Six million had been exterminated by Hitler's attempt at Jewish genocide. Millions more died from bombing, disease, and starvation. The United States lost over 290,000 in the fighting, but relatively few civilian casualties. Now that the Japanese had surrendered, and the American soldiers were coming home, there were wild celebrations in the streets all over the United States.

The Manhattan Project ended in 1947 after having spent 2 billion dollars to develop the atomic bomb. Los Alamos continued researching ways to improve nuclear weapons, but it was now under new authority. Congress formed the Atomic Energy Commission (AEC) in 1946 to bring nuclear energy under civilian control. Brigadier General Groves turned over the military's command of the Manhattan Project to the AEC's first chairman, David Lilienthal. Norris E. Bradbury succeeded J. Robert Oppenheimer as the director of Los Alamos.

Many scientists and government officials were in favor of going one step further. They foresaw a day when nuclear energy would be controlled by an international agency that could prevent the spread of nuclear weapons and an arms race. The AEC commissioned Bernard M. Baruch to formulate a plan for international cooperation on atomic energy. J. Robert Oppenheimer and other prominent scientists and policy makers aided Baruch. They proposed international controls on all aspects of nuclear energy including everything from the distribution of fissionable fuel to the operation of nuclear power plants. An important part of the Baruch plan was a call for the United States to destroy all its nuclear weapons. It also outlined a method of preventing other nations from acquiring nuclear weapons. Baruch presented the final plan to the United Nations in 1946. At the time the strategy was proposed, the United States thought that the rest of the nations of the world were years behind in developing their own nuclear weapons. The United States was surprised when Russia rejected the Baruch plan.

The Cold War

In 1949, the Soviet Union detonated their first atomic bomb, many years before anyone in the United States had expected them to accomplish this feat. Also in 1949, Klaus Fuchs was arrested in Great Britain for espionage. He subsequently confessed to giving the Soviets the secrets of the atomic bomb during his years of work at Los Alamos. After World War II, Russian troops remained in the Eastern European countries of Albania, Bulgaria, Czechoslovakia, Hungary, Romania, and Yugoslavia, effectively making them Russian satellites. The Soviets cut off all contact with the Western democracies. The Soviet "Iron Curtain" descended across Eastern Europe. The dream of international control of nuclear weapons was dead and the Cold War era had begun.

The United States began developing an even more powerful nuclear weapon to counter any potential Soviet threat. The first American hydrogen bomb was tested in 1952. This was a truly terrible weapon that was a thousand times more destructive than the atomic bombs dropped on Hiroshima and Nagasaki. The Russians followed by exploding their own hydrogen bomb in 1955. Each nation continued to improve its technology in a competitive arms race. As a result, the threat of nuclear war loomed over the earth. Ironically, it was the threat of mutual annihilation—the certainty that both sides would be destroyed—that kept either side from using its weapons in a nuclear showdown. Perhaps sobered by this fact, in 1970 the United States and the Soviet Union agreed to limit their stocks of nuclear weapons. This agreement paved the way for future arms limitation agreements with the eventual goal of the elimination of all nuclear weapons.

The Balance

After World War II, in a world under the shadow of nuclear devastation, nuclear energy found many beneficial uses. The first nuclear power plant began operation in 1957. Radioactive isotopes became extremely useful in the diagnosis and treatment of many medical conditions. But the balance between the pros and cons of nuclear technology is difficult to determine. In the early twenty-first century, Great Britain, France, China, India, and Pakistan possess nuclear weapons. Undoubtedly many more nations will acquire them. Despite the nuclear arms reduction agreements between the United States and Russia, the spread of these weapons of mass destruction has increased. Nuclear energy is now a global resource, and its use for good or ill is felt by all humankind. As Secretary of War Stimson wrote in 1946, "The focus of the problem does not lie in the atom; it resides in the hearts of men."[11]

Notes

1. Quoted in Ferenc Morton Szasz, *The Day the Sun Rose Twice.* Albuquerque: University of New Mexico Press, 1984, p. 89.
2. Edward Teller, *Memoirs.* Cambridge, MA: Perseus Publishing, 2001, p. 141.
3. Quoted in Richard Rhodes, *The Making of the Atom Bomb.* New York: Simon and Schuster, 1988, p. 243.
4. Quoted in Teller, *Memoirs*, p. 139.
5. Quoted in Teller, *Memoirs*, p. 143.
6. Quoted in Spencer R. Weart and Gertrud Weiss Szilard, eds., *Leo Szilard: His Version of the Facts.* Cambridge, MA: MIT Press, 1978, p. 95.
7. Quoted in Weart and Weiss Szilard, *Leo Szilard*, p. 95.
8. Quoted in Rhodes, *The Making of the Atom Bomb*, pp. 412–13.
9. Laura Fermi, *Atoms in the Family: My Life with Enrico Fermi.* University of Chicago Press, 1954, p. 181.
10. Quoted in Louie B. Young, *The Mystery of Matter.* New York: Oxford University Press, 1965, p. 182.
11. Quoted in Michael Blow, *The History of the Atomic Bomb.* New York: Harper and Row, p. 145.

Chapter 1

Discovery
of Fission

Chapter Preface

In 1903 the husband and wife team of Marie and Pierre Curie received the Nobel Prize for physics for their discovery of radium. Their research into radioactivity set the stage for a profound revolution in the way humans understand the makeup of their world. Albert Einstein in 1905 proved that matter was energy in his famous equation $E = mc^2$. This equation showed that when matter was transformed into energy, as it did in radioactivity, a very small amount of matter produced a very large amount of energy. By the early 1930s, the structure of the atom was known to be composed of a central nucleus made of positively charged protons and uncharged neutrons; negatively charged electrons orbited the nucleus of the atom like planets around the sun. By the late 1930s, scientists all over Europe were bombarding atoms with neutrons to find out more about radioactivity and the structure of the atom. In 1938, two German physicists, Otto Hahn and Fritz Strassmann bombarded a uranium atom with neutrons from a radium source. The neutron-bombarded uranium atoms produced energy and much lighter elements such as barium. This was a very surprising result. They did not understand how barium could be formed from uranium.

That same year, Hahn asked his colleague Lise Meitner to look at the strange results of their experiment. Meitner had fled to Sweden to escape Nazi persecution and had invited her nephew, physicist Otto Frisch, to spend the Christmas holidays with her in Sweden. As Frisch tells the story, during an evening walk in the snow, "we both sat down on a tree trunk . . . and started to calculate on scraps of paper." They knew that Niels Bohr had proposed that the nucleus of an atom could act like a drop of water that when stretched could break in two. As Frisch recalled, the calculations he and Meitner made that evening revealed that "the uranium nucleus might indeed resemble a very wobbly, unstable drop, ready to divide itself at the slightest provocation, such as the impact of a single neutron." They proved that the neutron-bombarded uranium had indeed split in two, producing energy, lighter elements, and more neutrons.

Niels Bohr, the Danish Nobel Prize–winning physicist, brought the news of this great breakthrough to America shortly after he received the information from Frisch. In the United States, Enrico Fermi, Leo Szilard, Eugene Wigner and Edward Teller, who had all recently left Europe to escape the Nazi anti-Semitism, duplicated and verified the fission experiments. These scientists became very concerned that Hitler might produce a bomb from this new source of nuclear energy. Eugene Wigner and Leo Szilard drafted a letter warning President Roosevelt of the destructive potential of an atom bomb. They took their letter to Albert Einstein to sign. Einstein's signature gave the letter the authority needed to get it on President Roosevelt's desk.

Roosevelt also got another report from a secret British government committee code named the MAUD Committee. This report stated that the atom bomb, through a huge industrial effort, could be produced before the war was over. Because of the letter from Einstein and the MAUD Report, Roosevelt committed the U.S. government to the enormous task of building the "bomb" shortly after the Japanese attacked Pearl Harbor on December 7, 1941.

Energy from Nuclei

Otto R. Frisch

Nuclear scientist Otto R. Frisch begins this account with a
basic lesson on what was known about the atom before 1938.
It was in that year that Frisch revolutionized science after visiting his aunt, Lise Meitner in Sweden during the Christmas
holidays. Meitner was also an eminent scientist who fled Nazi
Germany where she had been working with uranium and
radioactivity. While taking a walk in the snow, the two scientists made some calculations on scraps of paper that revealed
the tremendous amount of energy that would be released upon
splitting an atom. Frisch termed the atomic reaction "nuclear
fission." With this momentous discovery, Frisch went to work
in England and later the United States, using his knowledge of
fission to help develop the first atomic bomb. He collaborated
with such famous scientists as Niels Bohr, J. Robert Oppenheimer, and Edward Teller in nuclear experiments that would
be crucial in furthering the Manhattan Project. Frisch's
account is taken from his book *What Little I Remember.*
Despite the title, Frisch's memory is vivid and his explanation
of the science of fission is lucid and understandable.

D id I say that all nuclei had weights that were multiples
of that of a hydrogen nucleus? That is not quite true;
most of them are about 1% lighter than that, and therein lies
the secret of nuclear (often called 'atomic') energy. When
protons come together to form heavier nuclei their joint
mass becomes less by an amount m, and a lot of energy E is
set free, following Einstein's formulae $E = mc^2$. The factor

Excerpted from *What Little I Remember*, by Otto R. Frisch (New York: Cambridge University Press, 1979). Copyright © 1979 by Cambridge University Press. Reprinted with
permission.

c^2 (speed of light multiplied by itself) is very large, so a minute amount of mass corresponds to a lot of energy; for instance the mass of a paper-clip is equivalent to the entire energy a small town uses during a day.

Energy is measured in a variety of units: kWh (kilowatt-hours) on your electricity meter, Btu (British thermal units) for the gas man, and so on. Those are man-size units, much too large for a single nucleus. For them the common unit is the MeV (a million electron-volt, but usually we say 'an em-meevee'). It is the energy of motion which an electron (or a proton) acquires when it is accelerated by a voltage of a million volts. An alpha particle has typically 5 to 10 MeV; to keep a watch going needs several million times as much energy every second.

Einstein's formula was put to the test in the 1930s by measuring the energy of the particles (e.g. protons) set free in 'atom splitting'. The collision of two nuclei caused the nucleons to be rearranged so as to form two new nuclei; when those were both of a kind found in nature it was possible to compare the masses of the nuclei before and after the collision and check the mass difference against the energy set free.

Nuclear Fire in the Sun

What do those masses tell us? Well, for one thing, they tell us why the sun keeps shining. If you could dive into the huge white-hot ball of not-quite-pure hydrogen which we call the sun you would find rapidly rising pressure and temperature until near the centre the temperature is around ten million degrees Centigrade. At such heat the hydrogen nuclei move so fast (about 500 km/sec) that they occasionally collide despite their mutual electric repulsion. There are traces of other elements, which complicate what happens; Hans Bethe, whom I later met in Los Alamos, was the first to work out a possible mechanism for this process in detail. To cut the story short, the main outcome is simply that helium nuclei are formed, one from four hydrogen nuclei (two of which are changed from protons into neutrons), and each hydrogen nucleus gives up 7 MeV in that process. In this 'nuclear fire' about a million times more energy is produced than in ordinary (chemical) fire, for instance when hydrogen burns by combining with oxygen. Even so the amount of hydrogen the sun has to burn to keep shining is stupendous: about ten billion tons every second! But the sun is big: in the four billion years since the Earth became solid the sun has used up only a fraction of its hydrogen. . . .

Here we have some simple clues. Light nuclei contain as many neutrons as protons. The reason is a variant of Pauli's housing rule: two protons, spinning oppositely, can inhabit one quantum state, together with two neutrons behaving the same way. The first complete family of that kind is indeed the helium nucleus, rare on Earth but exceedingly common in the sun and the stars. But then why do heavier nuclei contain relatively more neutrons? Why is the ratio of neutrons to protons about 1.2:1 for copper, 1.4:1 for iodine and 1.6:1 for uranium? Because protons are bad club members: they are electrically charged and hence repel each other, and it makes a heavy nucleus more stable if some of them are turned into neutrons even though, as a result, they may have to move into higher quantum states. Nuclei with too few or too many protons adjust the ratio after a while by sending out an electron or a positron. . . .

Subatomic Forces

But in the heaviest nuclei, even when the ratio of neutrons to protons is at its optimum, the protons are still under pressure from their mutual repulsion. Then why don't they just get pushed out? In fact what is holding nuclei together? The protons repel each other, and the neutrons—being electrically neutral—cannot be held by electric forces. Gravity? Many million times too weak.

Today we know that any two nucleons attract each other very strongly, but only when they are very close together. We have no special name for that attraction; we call it simply 'the nuclear force'. It is more like a kind of stickiness, and we even think we know something about the nature of the glue. It acts only between nucleons in the same nucleus, except for a brief moment when two nuclei collide.

But the heavy nuclei have a trick to unload some of their quarrelsome protons. Two protons can combine with two neutrons and emigrate as a family; the 28 MeV which are gained (as in the process that keeps the sun shining!) serve to pay for the exit visa, as it were. In classical mechanics such a process would be impossible; like mountaineers trying to climb out of a crater on an insufficient supply of food, they would find that their energy gives out before they reach the rim and overcome the pull of the other nucleons.

Classical physics is adamant about that, but the laws of quantum mechanics are more flexible. They allow our subatomic mountaineer to 'tunnel' through the crater wall, as some physicists like to put it. Or you may imagine that two protons and two neutrons use Heisenberg's uncertainty principle to borrow some energy, to be repaid after they have left the nucleus and become a helium nucleus, a newborn alpha particle, rapidly driven away by the electric repulsion of the remaining nucleus, sliding down the outer crater wall as it were. But such a loan is granted only after uncounted billions of applications. . . .

Christmas with Lise Meitner

Until 1938 nobody dreamt that there was yet another way for a heavy nucleus to react to the mutual repulsion of its many protons, namely by dividing itself into two roughly equal halves. It was mere chance that I became involved in the discovery of that 'nuclear fission', which for the first time showed a way to make huge numbers of nuclei give up their hidden energy; the way to the atom bomb and to atomic power.

The occupation of Austria in March 1938 changed my aunt, the physicist Lise Meitner—technically—from an Austrian into a German. She had acquired fame by many years' work in Germany, but now had to fear dismissal as a descendant of a Jewish family. Moreover, there was a rumour that scientists might not be allowed to leave Germany; so she was persuaded—or perhaps stampeded—into leaving at very short notice, assisted by friends in Holland, and in the autumn she accepted an invitation to work in Stockholm, at the Nobel Institute led by Manne Siegbahn. I had always kept the habit of celebrating Christmas with her in Berlin; this time she was invited to spend Christmas with Swedish friends in the small town of Kungälv (near Gothenburg), and she asked me to join her there. That was the most momentous visit of my whole life.

Let me first explain that Lise Meitner had been working in Berlin with the chemist Otto Hahn for about thirty years, and during the last three years they had been bombarding uranium with neutrons and studying the radioactive substances that were formed. Fermi, who had first done that, thought he had made 'transuranic' elements—that is, elements beyond uranium (the heaviest element then known to the chemists), and Hahn the chemist was delighted to have a lot of new elements to study. But Lise Meitner saw how difficult it was to account for the large number of different substances formed, and things got even more complicated when some were found (in Paris) that were apparently lighter than uranium. Just before Lise Meitner left Germany, Hahn had confirmed that this was so, and that three of those substances behaved chemically like radium. It was hard to see how radium—four places below uranium—could be formed by the impact of a neutron, and Lise Meitner wrote to Hahn, imploring him not to publish that incomprehensible result until he was completely sure of it. Accordingly Hahn, together with his collaborator, the chemist Fritz Strassmann, decided to carry out thorough tests in order to make quite sure that those substances were indeed of the same chemical nature as radium.

When I came out of my hotel room after my first night in Kungälv I found Lise Meitner studying a letter from Hahn and obviously worried by it. I wanted to tell her of a new experiment I was planning, but she wouldn't listen; I had to read that letter. Its content was indeed so startling that I was at first inclined to be sceptical. Hahn and Strassmann had found that those three substances were not radium, chemically speaking; indeed they had found it impossible to separate them from the barium which, routinely, they had added in order to facilitate the chemical separations. They had come to the conclusion, reluctantly and with hesitation, that they were isotopes of barium.

Was it just a mistake? No, said Lise Meitner; Hahn was too good a chemist for that. But how could barium be formed from uranium? No larger fragments than protons or helium nuclei (alpha particles) had ever been chipped away from nuclei, and to chip off a large number not nearly enough energy was available. Nor was it possible that the uranium nucleus could have been cleaved right across. A nucleus was not like a brittle solid that can be cleaved or broken; George Gamov had suggested early on, and Bohr had given good arguments that a nucleus was much more like a liquid drop. Perhaps a drop could divide itself into two smaller drops in a more gradual manner, by first becoming elongated, then constricted, and finally being torn rather than broken in two? We knew that there were strong forces that would resist such a process, just as the surface tension of an ordinary liquid drop tends to resist its division into two smaller ones. But the nuclei differed from ordinary drops in one important way: they were electrically charged, and that was known to counteract the surface tension.

Calculations in the Snow

At that point we both sat down on a tree trunk (all that discussion had taken place while we walked through the wood in the snow, I with my skis on, Lise Meitner making good her claim that she could walk just as fast without), and started to calculate on scraps of paper. The charge of a uranium nucleus, we found, was indeed large enough to overcome the effect of the surface tension almost completely; so the uranium nucleus might indeed resemble a very wobbly, unstable drop, ready to divide itself at the slightest provocation, such as the impact of a single neutron.

But there was another problem. After separation, the two

drops would be driven apart by their mutual electric repulsion and would acquire high speed and hence a very large energy, about 200 MeV in all; where could that energy come from? Fortunately Lise Meitner remembered the empirical formula for computing the masses of nuclei and worked out that the two nuclei formed by the division of a uranium nucleus together would be lighter than the original uranium nucleus by about one-fifth the mass of a proton. Now whenever mass disappears energy is created, according to Einstein's formula $E = mc^2$, and one-fifth of a proton mass was just equivalent to 200 MeV. So here was the source for that energy; it all fitted!

A couple of days later I travelled back to Copenhagen in considerable excitement. I was keen to submit our speculations—it wasn't really more at the time—to Bohr, who was just about to leave for the U.S.A. He had only a few minutes for me; but I had hardly begun to tell him when he smote his forehead with his hand and exclaimed: 'Oh what idiots we all have been! Oh but this is wonderful! This is just as it must be! Have you and Lise Meitner written a paper about it?' Not yet, I said, but we would at once; and Bohr promised not to talk about it before the paper was out. Then he went off to catch his boat.

"Nuclear Fission" Is Named

The paper was composed by several long-distance telephone calls, Lise Meitner having returned to Stockholm in the meantime. I asked an American biologist who was working with Hevesy what they call the process by which single cells divide in two; 'fission', he said, so I used the term 'nuclear fission' in that paper. Placzek was sceptical; couldn't I do some experiments to show the existence of those fast-moving fragments of the uranium nucleus? Oddly enough that thought hadn't occurred to me, but now I quickly set to work, and the experiment (which was really very easy) was done in two days, and a short note about it was sent off to *Nature* together with the other note I had composed over the telephone with Lise Meitner. This time—with no [physicist

Patrick] Blackett to speed things up—about five weeks passed before *Nature* printed those notes.

In the meantime the paper by Hahn and Strassmann arrived in the U.S.A., and several teams did within hours the same experiment which I had done on Placzek's challenge. A few days later Bohr heard about my own experiments, not from me (I wanted to get more results before wasting money on a transatlantic telegram!) but from his son Hans to whom I had casually talked about my work. Bohr responded with a barrage of telegrams, asking for details and proposing further experiments, and he worked hard to convince journalists that the decisive experiment had been done by Frisch in Copenhagen before the Americans. . . .

Chain Reaction

In all this excitement we had missed the most important point: the chain reaction. It was Christian Møller, a Danish colleague, who first suggested to me that the fission fragments (the two freshly formed nuclei) might contain enough surplus energy each to eject a neutron or two; each of these might cause another fission and generate more neutrons. By such a 'chain reaction' the neutrons would multiply in uranium like rabbits in a meadow! My immediate answer was that in that case no uranium ore deposits could exist: they would have blown up long ago by the explosive multiplication of neutrons in them. But I quickly saw that my argument was too naive; ores contained lots of other elements which might swallow up the neutrons; and the seams were perhaps thin, and then most of the neutrons would escape. So, from Møller's remark the exciting vision arose that by assembling enough pure uranium (with appropriate care!) one might start a controlled chain reaction and liberate nuclear energy on a scale that really mattered. Many others independently had the same thought, as I soon found out. Of course the spectre of a bomb—an uncontrolled chain reaction—was there as well; but for a while anyhow, it looked as though it need not frighten us. That complacency was based on an argument by Bohr, which was subtle but appeared quite sound.

The Importance of Uranium-235

In a paper on the theory of fission that he wrote in the U.S.A. with John Wheeler, Bohr concluded that most of the neutrons emitted by the fission fragments would be too slow to cause fission of the chief isotope, uranium-238. Yet slow neutrons did cause fission; this he attributed to the rare isotope uranium-235. If he was right the only chance of getting a chain reaction with natural uranium was to arrange for the neutrons to be slowed down, whereby their effect on uranium-235 is increased. But in that manner one could not get a violent explosion; slow neutrons take their time, and even if the conditions for rapid neutron multiplication were created this would at best (or at worst!) cause the assembly to heat up and disperse itself, with only a minute fraction of its nuclear energy liberated.

All this was quite correct, and the development of nuclear reactors followed on the whole the lines which Bohr foresaw. What he did not foresee was the fanatical ingenuity of the allied physicists and engineers, driven by the fear that Hitler might develop the decisive weapon before they did. I was in England when the war broke out, and in Los Alamos when I saw Bohr again. By that time it was clear that there were even two ways for getting an effective nuclear explosion: either through the separation of the highly fissile isotope uranium-235 or by using the new element plutonium, formed in a nuclear reactor.

Publishing the Secret of Fission

Leo Szilard

In 1939, Leo Szilard, a physicist who had just immigrated to the United States from Hungary, still had his doubts about sustaining a chain reaction during the splitting of a uranium atom. He then heard of the discovery of nuclear fission and from this realized that splitting the uranium atom could produce a chain reaction and a resulting explosion. Szilard discussed his conclusions with other scientists who were working on atomic research such as Frédéric Joliot in France and Enrico Fermi who had recently immigrated to the United States from Italy.

When Fermi, working at Columbia University in New York, performed an experiment that confirmed the existence of the fission reaction, Szilard was excited and yet concerned. He feared that if the Nazis gained knowledge on how to split the atom, the world would be in great danger. He thus opposed the publication of any papers on the fission experiments. Fermi took the opposite position, saying that suppression of information was unthinkable in a democracy. While this debate was going on among a host of scientists in America, Joliot, in France, published his findings around March 1939 and made the Americans' argument moot. Still, Szilard resisted till the last, and his stance on secrecy was to be mimicked by the American government in the ensuing years during the development of the bomb. Szilard's recollection of these events is taken from the book *Leo Szilard: His Version of the Facts,* published in 1978.

Excerpted from *Leo Szilard: His Version of the Facts: Selected Recollections and Correspondence*, vol. II, edited by Spencer R. Weart and Gertrud Weiss Szilard (New York: Halliday Lithograph Corporation, 1980). Copyright © 1980 by Gertrud Weiss Szilard. Reprinted with permission.

I was still intrigued with the possibility of a chain reaction, and for that reason I was interested in elements which became radioactive when they were bombarded by neutrons and where there were more radioactive isotopes than there should have been. In particular I was interested in indium. I went up to Rochester [New York] and stayed there for two weeks and made some experiments on indium which finally cleared up this mystery. It turned out that indium is not unstable and that the phenomenon observed could be explained without assuming that indium is split by neutrons.

At that point I abandoned the idea of a chain reaction and I abandoned the idea of looking for elements which could sustain a chain reaction. I wrote a letter to the British Admiralty suggesting that the patent which had been applied for should be withdrawn because I couldn't make the process work. Before that letter reached them, I learned of the discovery of fission. This was early in January when I visited Mr. [Eugene] Wigner in Princeton, who was ill with jaundice.

Wigner told me of [Otto] Hahn's discovery. Hahn found that uranium breaks into two parts when it absorbs a neutron; this is the process which we call fission. When I heard this I saw immediately that these fragments, being heavier than corresponds to their charge, must emit neutrons, and if enough neutrons are emitted in this fission process, then it should be, of course, possible to sustain a chain reaction. All the things which H.G. Wells predicted appeared suddenly real to me.

At that time it was already clear, not only to me but to many other people—certainly it was clear to Wigner—that we were at the threshold of another world war. And so it seemed to us urgent to set up experiments which would show whether in fact neutrons are emitted in the fission process of uranium. I thought that if neutrons are in fact emitted in fission, this fact should be kept secret from the Germans. So I was very eager to contact Joliot and to contact Fermi, the two men who were most likely to think of this possibility.

I was still in Princeton and staying at Wigner's apartment—Wigner was in the hospital with jaundice. I got up in the morning and wanted to go out. It was raining cats and dogs. I said, "My God, I am going to catch a cold!" Because at that time, the first years I was in America, each time I got wet I invariably caught a bad cold. However, I had no rubbers with me, so I had no choice, I just had to go out. I got wet and came home with a high fever, so I was not able to contact Fermi. As I got ready to go back to New York, I opened the drawer to take my things out and saw there were Wigner's rubbers standing. I could have taken Wigner's rubbers and avoided the cold. But as it was I was laid up with fever for about a week or ten days. In the meantime, Fermi also thought of the possibility of a neutron emission and the possibility of a chain reaction and he went to a private meeting in Washington and talked about these things. Since it was a private meeting, the cat was not entirely out of the bag, but its tail was sticking out.

Possibility of a Bomb

When I recovered I went to see [Isidor Isaac] Rabi [professor of physics at Columbia University], and Rabi told me that Fermi had similar ideas and that he had talked about them in Washington. Fermi was not in, so I told Rabi to please talk to Fermi and say that these things ought to be kept secret because it's very likely that neutrons are emitted, this may lead to a chain reaction, and this may lead to the construction of bombs. So Rabi said he would and I went back home to bed in the King's Crown Hotel. A few days later I got up and again went to see Rabi, and I said to him, "Did you talk to Fermi?" Rabi said, "Yes, I did." I said, "What did Fermi say?" Rabi said, "Fermi said 'Nuts!'" So I said, "Why did he say 'Nuts!'?" and Rabi said, "Well, I don't know, but he is in and we can ask him." So we went over to Fermi's office, and Rabi said to Fermi, "Look, Fermi, I told you what Szilard thought and you said 'Nuts!' and Szilard wants to know why you said 'Nuts!'" So Fermi said, "Well . . . there is the remote possibility that neutrons may be emitted in the fission of uranium and then of course perhaps a chain reaction can be made." Rabi said, "What do you mean by 'remote possibility'?" and Fermi said, "Well, ten per cent." Rabi said, "Ten per cent is not a remote possibility if it means that we may die of it. If I have pneumonia and the doctor tells me that there is a remote possibility that I might die, and it's ten per cent, I get excited about it."

From the very beginning the line was drawn; the difference between Fermi's position throughout this and mine was marked on the first day we talked about it. We both wanted to be conservative, but Fermi thought that the conservative thing was to play down the possibility that this may happen, and I thought the conservative thing was to assume that it would happen and take all the necessary precautions. I then went and wrote a letter to Joliot, in which I told Joliot that we were discussing here the possibility of neutron emission of uranium in the fission process and the possibility of a chain reaction, and that I personally felt that these things should be discussed privately among the physicists in England, France, and America, and that there should be no publication on this topic if it should turn out that neutrons are, in fact, emitted and that a chain reaction might be possible. This letter was dated February 2, 1939. I then sent a telegram to England asking them to send a block of beryllium which I had had made in Germany with the kind of experiments in mind which I now was actually going to perform.

A Simple Experiment

Such a block of beryllium can be used to produce slow neutrons, because if you put radium in the middle of it, under the influence of the gamma rays of radium the beryllium splits and gives off slow neutrons. If uranium in the process of fission, which can be caused by slow neutrons, emits fast neutrons, these fast neutrons can be distinguished from the neutrons of the source by virtue of their higher energy.

There was at Columbia University some equipment which was very suitable for these experiments. This equipment was built by Dr. Walter Zinn, who was doing experiments with it. All we needed to do was to get a gram of radium, get a block of beryllium, expose a piece of uranium to the neutrons which come from beryllium, and then see by means of the ionization chamber which Zinn had built whether fast neutrons were emitted in the process. Such an experiment need not take more than an hour or two to perform, once the equipment has been built and if you have the neutron source. But of course we had no radium.

So, I first tried to talk to some of my wealthy friends, but they wanted to know just how sure I was that this would work. Finally I talked to one of my not-so-wealthy friends. He was a successful inventor, he was not poor but he was not exactly wealthy. His name is Benjamin Liebowitz. He derived some income from royalties. I told him what this was all about, and he said, "How much money do you need?" I said, "Well, I'd like to borrow $2,000." He took out his checkbook, he wrote out a check, I cashed the check, I rented the gram of radium, and in the meantime the beryllium block arrived from England. With this radium and beryllium I turned up at Columbia and, having talked to Zinn, said to the head of the department, "I would like to have permission to do some experiments." I was given permission to do experiments for three months. I don't know what caused this caution, because they knew me quite well; but perhaps the idea was a little too fantastic to be entirely respectable. And once we had the radium and the beryllium it took us just one afternoon to see the neutrons. Mr. Zinn and I performed this experiment.

[On March 3, 1939] everything was ready and all we had to do was to turn a switch, lean back, and watch the screen of a television tube. If flashes of light appeared on the screen, that would mean that neutrons were emitted in the fission process of uranium and this in turn would mean that the large-scale liberation of atomic energy was just around the corner. We turned the switch and we saw the flashes. We watched them for a little while and then we switched everything off and went home. That night there was very little doubt in my mind that the world was headed for grief.

At that point I thought that from this point on there should be no difficulty in obtaining financial support for this work. But in this I was quite mistaken.

In the meantime Fermi, who had independently thought of this possibility, had set up an experiment. His did not at first work so well, because he used a neutron source which emitted fast neutrons, but then he borrowed our neutron source and his experiment, which was of a completely different design, also showed the neutrons.

Soon after we had discovered the neutron emission of uranium, Wigner came to New York and we met—Fermi and I and Wigner—in the office of Dr. Pegram [head of Columbia's physics department]. Wigner said that this was such a serious business that we could not assume the responsibility for handling it; we must contact and inform the government. Pegram said that we could do that; he knew Charles Edison, who was the assistant secretary of the navy. He told Edison that Fermi would be in Washington the next day and would be glad to meet with a committee and explain certain matters which might be of interest to the navy. Fermi went there. He was received by a committee. He told in his cautious way the story of uranium and what potential possibilities were involved. But there the matter ended. I got an echo of this through [physicist] Merle Tuve. Ross Gunn, who was an adviser to the navy and who attended this conference, telephoned Tuve and asked him, "Who is this man Fermi? What kind of a man is he? Is he a Fascist or what? What is he?" Nothing came of this.

"Shall We Publish This?"

And now there came the question: Shall we publish this? There were intensive discussions about this. Zinn and I, and Fermi and [Herbert] Anderson [a student working with Fermi], each sent a paper to the *Physical Review*, a letter to the editor. But we requested that these publications be delayed for a little while until we could decide whether we wanted to keep these things secret or whether we would permit them to be published. Throughout this time I kept in close touch with Wigner and with Edward Teller, who was in Washington. I went down to Washington; Fermi also went down to Washington on some other business, I forget what it was, and Teller and Fermi and I got together to discuss whether or not these things should be published. Both Teller and I thought that they should not. Fermi thought that they should. But after a long discussion, Fermi took the position that after all this was a democracy; if the majority was against publication, he would abide by the wish of the majority, and he said that he would go back to New York and advise the head of the department, Dean Pegram, to ask that publication of these papers be indefinitely delayed.

While we were still in Washington we learned that Joliot and his coworkers had sent a note to *Nature*, reporting the discovery that neutrons are emitted in the fission of uranium and indicating that this might lead to a chain reaction. At this point Fermi said that in this case we were going to publish now everything. I was not willing to do that, and I said that even though Joliot had published this, this was just a first step, and that if we persisted in not publishing, Joliot would have to come around; otherwise he would be at a disadvantage, because we would know his results and he would not know of our results. However, from that moment on Fermi was adamant that withholding publication made no sense. I still did not want to yield and so we agreed that we would put up this matter for a decision to the head of the physics department, Professor Pegram.

A telegram was sent by [physicist Victor] Weisskopf to [Hans von] Halban in Joliot's laboratory reminding Joliot of my letter and advising him that we were approaching the British physicists. Another telegram was sent by Weisskopf to [physics professor Patrick] Blackett in England suggesting that the British withhold all publications on this subject. A letter was sent by Wigner to [physicist Paul] Dirac in Cambridge, England, to the same effect. Blackett cabled to Weisskopf that the collaboration of the Royal Society could be expected, but Joliot's reply was not satisfactory. Joliot's cable pointed out that articles had appeared in the American press in February which were based on statements by

[Richard B.] Roberts in Tuve's laboratory and let the cat out of the bag. To this cable of Joliot I replied that we had in the meantime secured the collaboration of Tuve's laboratory and I urged Joliot to agree to a collaboration in this matter. The answer of Joliot to my telegram was negative.

The Americans Decide to Publish

After Joliot's final refusal to collaborate, all my colleagues at Columbia University expressed themselves in favor of publishing our papers. I continued to take the stand that irrespective of Joliot's policy, we ought not to publish our own work. Pegram, the head of the department, was undecided. It seemed impossible to reconcile the two opposing views, and Professor I. Rabi at Columbia, who was not himself involved in this work, gave me a friendly warning that if I continued to take such an irreconcilable stand, I would probably be left without facilities for further work at Columbia. At the suggestion of Fermi, we finally agreed to leave the decision up to Pegram, the head of the department. Pegram hesitated for a while to make this decision, and after a few weeks he finally came and said that he had decided that we should now publish everything.

He later told me why he decided this—and so many decisions were based on the wrong premises. Rabi was concerned about my stand because he said that everybody was opposed to withholding publication, only I wanted it in the Columbia group. This would make my position difficult, in the end impossible, and he thought that I ought to yield on this. According to what Pegram told me, Rabi had visited Urbana and found that [physicist Maurice] Goldhaber in Urbana knew of our research at Columbia; from this Rabi concluded that these results were already known as far as Urbana, Illinois, and there was no point in keeping them secret. The fact was that I was in constant communication with Goldhaber; I wrote him of these results, and he was pledged to secrecy. He talked to Rabi because of course Rabi was part of the Columbia operation. So on this false premise, the decision was made that we should publish.

Warning of the Dangers of Nuclear Technology

Edward Teller

Edward Teller was born in Budapest, Hungary, in 1908. As a young scientist, he immigrated to the United States in 1935. By 1939, Teller was working with Leo Szilard and Enrico Fermi on the first nuclear chain reaction project. In the following selection, Teller gives a vivid portrait of these important men who were involved in these momentous discoveries. He shows how the brilliant and sometimes difficult scientists interacted. Teller often served as an intermediary between these great scientific minds who otherwise might not have been able to work together. In telling this story, he also outlines the progress of the significant early discoveries relating to the splitting of the atom.

Teller realized early on the dangers of atomic fission. He was one of the first to try to alert the U.S. government that an enemy power with nuclear technology could pose a terrible threat to the nation. Teller accompanied Szilard on a historic visit to Albert Einstein in Long Island, New York. There, Teller witnessed Einstein signing the letter to President Roosevelt informing him that nuclear fission could produce a powerful new bomb and warning that Nazi Germany might also develop this same capability. This letter prompted Roosevelt to take action and led to the funding of the Manhattan Project and the building of the first atomic bomb six years later.

Excerpted from *Memoirs: A Twentieth-Century Journey in Science and Politics*, by Edward Teller (Cambridge, MA: Perseus Publishing, 2001). Copyright © 2001 by Edward Teller. Reprinted with permission.

Teller worked on both the atomic and hydrogen bombs at Los Alamos and was credited along with Stanislaw Ulam with the invention of the U.S. hydrogen bomb. This account is taken from his 2001 book, *Memoirs: A Twentieth-Century Journey in Science and Politics.*

In 1932, Fermi had begun to bombard, systematically, all the elements with neutrons, a process that produces radioactive substances. He found that if a lightweight element captures a neutron, it produces a single radioactive element with a specific half-life. Heavier elements that have three or more naturally occurring isotopes may produce several radioactive isotopes. If a heavier element has fewer than three isotopes, neutron capture usually leads to one radioactive isotope, which then decays and may produce another radioactive substance.

During my visit to Copenhagen in 1935, I happened to hear a talk at Bohr's Institute given by Lise Meitner, an excellent physicist who was then working at the Kaiser Wilhelm Institute in Berlin. She was bothered by an inconsistency in Fermi's results. "Something odd," she said, "is going on with uranium. Why does uranium simultaneously produce dozens of radioactive substances when it should produce only one?" Fermi's interpretation of the multiple radioactivities was that new elements (called transuranics because they are heavier than uranium) had been produced. Meitner noted the oddity, but she did not challenge Fermi's interpretation.

In 1938, Fermi won the Nobel Prize for his work. He had become more and more uneasy about remaining in Mussolini's Italy. His father-in-law was a Jew who had retired from the Italian navy as an admiral. That a Jew held so high a rank accurately suggests that historically anti-Semitism was not endemic in Italy. But the Berlin-Rome axis had introduced the Nazi form of anti-Semitism. That completed Fermi's list of reasons why he had to take his family out of Italy. Leaving everything behind, the Fermis went to Stockholm to accept the Nobel Prize; they used the prize money to travel on to New York, where Enrico settled in as a professor at Columbia.

As 1939 began, I was looking forward to seeing Fermi at the fifth theoretical conference at George Washington University, scheduled for January 19–20. Much to Geo's [theoretical physicist George Gamow] and my pleasure, Niels Bohr, who had just arrived from Copenhagen to work for a few weeks at Princeton, was also going to participate in the program.

Bohr arrived at Gamow's home late in the afternoon the day before the conference began. An hour or so later, Geo called me in great agitation: "Bohr has gone crazy. He says uranium splits." That was all of Geo's message. Within half an hour, I realized what Bohr was talking about. If the uranium nucleus (the heaviest of the naturally occurring elements) were to split, it could split in a variety of ways. That would account for the many simultaneously produced radioactivities.

Meitner's question had been answered, the tool Szilárd had wished for was now available, and Nazi Germany might well develop a devastating new weapon. My sleep that night was uneasy. . .

Accidents of History

That the secret of fission had eluded everybody for all those years amazed me. . . . In one of his experiments, Fermi had bombarded uranium with neutrons to observe the alpha particles that picked up extra energy from the neutrons. Because he carried out the experiment in a Geiger counter, the highly energetic fission fragments would have been unmistakable. But Fermi was a very careful experimenter. He covered his uranium with a thin sheet of inert material to stop the normal alpha particles (without the extra energy) in which he was not interested. That sheet also stopped the fission products, which had a short range but extremely high energy-density. Had Fermi forgotten to cover his sample even once, fission would have been discovered years earlier.

Physicist Paul Scherrer in Zurich had an even closer encounter with the discovery. He bombarded thorium . . . with neutrons and saw the fission fragments that Meitner and [her nephew Otto] Frisch had identified. But Scherrer wouldn't believe his eyes. He thought his Geiger counter was malfunctioning. What wasn't expected wasn't seen!

In 1939, I did not realize how fortunate it was that those slight changes in an experiment in Rome or Zurich did not occur. If fission had been discovered in 1933, work on the topic in Germany and the Soviet Union—two nations that took the military applications of science seriously—would have been well advanced by 1939. Under different conditions, the United States probably would not have been the first nation to possess nuclear explosives. Fermi, Scherrer, and Szilárd, in their different ways, had a profound and beneficent influence on history.

When our conference was over and [my wife] Mici and I had collapsed agreeably into a well-deserved rest, the telephone rang: "This is Szilárd. I am at the Union Station. Please pick me up." Mici revived and came along, after making me promise not to invite Szilárd to stay with us. (Szilárd was a demanding houseguest, and Mici had worked hard during the conference.) But when we met him in front of the station, her first words to him were: "Would you like to stay with us?" Szilárd accepted with pleasure.

When we got home, Mici took Szilárd to our small guest room. He sat on the bed, bounced a few times, and said in an unusually cautious voice: "I have tried to sleep on this bed before. The mattress is quite hard. Is there a hotel nearby?" Mici, with a bright smile, pointed out the window. "There is the Wardman Park Hotel (now the Sheraton Park) in our backyard." Half a century later, Mici was still boasting about her tact on that occasion.

Szilárd had found a position at Columbia but had not been invited to the conference (because low-temperature physics was not one of his interests). Nonetheless, he had heard the news about fission; it had spread through the world of physicists like wildfire. He was not surprised to hear that, apart from confirming fission, none of us at the conference had proceeded further. But Szilárd started where the conference had left off. "Now," he reiterated, "nuclear energy and nuclear explosions are feasible, provided only that, on the average, more than one neutron is emitted in the fission process."

Szilárd began designing an experiment to find out whether fission does produce additional neutrons. About a month later, I was playing a Mozart sonata on our landlady's substandard piano with an acquaintance who was a good violinist. In the middle of the piece, Szilárd called from New York. In those days, long distance calls were unusual events at our house, but the message was more so: "I found the neutrons." When I returned to the piano, I knew that the world might change in a radical manner. The prospect of harnessing nuclear energy seemed chillingly real. . . .

Peacemaker Between Szilárd and Fermi

During the summer of 1939, I taught summer school at Columbia. I lectured graduate students, but I was invited primarily as a consultant-peacemaker on the Fermi-Szilárd chain reaction project. Fermi and Szilárd both had asked me to work with them. They were barely speaking to each other.

Temperamentally, the two men were almost opposites. Fermi was an exceptionally conservative man; scientifically he was careful, methodical, and responsible. Szilárd was imaginative and flamboyant and lacked even an approximation of the qualities Fermi possessed and valued highly. Fermi seldom said anything that he couldn't demonstrate. Szilárd seldom said anything that was not startling and new. Fermi was humble and self-effacing. Szilárd could not talk without giving orders. Only if they had an intermediary could they be in contact with each other for any length of time. So Mici and I spent the summer in New York City as the missing link in the Fermi-Szilárd communication chain. Because I admired and enjoyed working with both men and they were comfortable with me, I became a conduit of information, able to solve problems between them unobtrusively, sometimes even before they occurred.

[German Nobel Prize–winning physicist Werner] Heisenberg visited us during that summer. My respect for him usually kept me from inquiring about personal matters. But this time, with the hope for appeasement in shambles and war around the corner, I asked Heisenberg why he didn't stay in the United States. His answer was simple and straightforward: "Even if my brother steals a silver spoon, he is still my brother." I would have liked to change his mind, but I could not find a way to present my arguments that would have fit our relationship.

In retrospect, it is clear that he, not yet forty years old, made a decision that marked a turning point in his life, before he realized how much more than a silver spoon was involved. Heisenberg had confirmed my belief that understanding was the most important function and the highest pleasure that life offered. During the years that followed, he endured profound and painful difficulties.

A Trip to See Einstein

My other memorable guest that summer, Leo Szilárd, visited often. One day he asked, "Could you drive me to the end of Long Island to see Einstein tomorrow?" Szilárd accomplished the extraordinary, but he had not learned to drive. I told him I could. I knew the general purpose of the visit. Szilárd was determined to alert the government to the possibility of a fission weapon. He had decided to write President Roosevelt a letter, and he expected it to be read because he had convinced his more famous friend, Albert Einstein, to sign it.

So one day early in August, we set out for Long Island. Unfortunately, Szilárd knew only Einstein's general whereabouts, not his address. Once we were in the right neighborhood, we began inquiring about the famous professor, with no result. Finally, we asked a little girl with long braids, about eight years old. She had never heard of Professor Einstein, but she knew a nice old man with long white hair. We were, she told us, almost in front of his house.

Einstein invited us in for tea, and afterwards, Szilárd produced a typewritten letter from his pocket.

Old Grove Road
Nassau Point
Peconic, Long Island
August 2, 1939
F.D. Roosevelt
President of the United States
White House
Washington, D.C.
Sir:

Some recent work by E. Fermi and L. Szilárd, which has been communicated to me in manuscript, leads me to expect that the element uranium may be turned into a new and important source of energy in the immediate future. Certain aspects of the situation which has arisen seem to call for watchfulness and, if necessary, quick action on the part of the Administration. I believe, therefore that it is my duty to bring to your attention the following facts and recommendations.

In the course of the last four months it has been made probable—through the work of [Frédéric] Joliot in France as well as Fermi and Szilárd in America—that it may become possible to set up a nuclear chain reaction in a large mass of uranium, by which vast amounts of power and large quantities of new radium-like elements would be generated. Now it appears almost certain that this could be achieved in the immediate future.

This new phenomenon would also lead to the construction of bombs, and it is conceivable—though much less certain—that extremely powerful bombs of a new type, carried by boat and exploded in a port, might very well destroy the whole port together with some of the surrounding territory. However, such bombs might very well prove to be too heavy for transportation by air.

The United States has only very poor ores of uranium in moderate quantities. There is some good ore in Canada and the former Czechoslovakia, while the most important source of uranium is the Belgian Congo.

In view of this situation you may think it desirable to have some permanent contact maintained between the Administration and the group of physicists working on chain reaction in America. One possible way of achieving this might be for you to entrust with this task a person who has your confidence and who could perhaps serve in an unofficial capacity. His task might comprise the following:

a) to approach Government departments, keep them informed of the further development, and put forward recommendations for Government action, giving particular attention to the problem of securing a supply of uranium ore for the United States.

b) to speed up the experimental work which is at present being carried on within the limits of the budgets of university laboratories, by providing funds if such be required, through his contacts with private persons who are willing to make contributions for this cause, and perhaps also by obtaining the cooperation of industrial laboratories which have the necessary equipment.

I understand that Germany has actually stopped the sale of uranium from the Czechoslovakian mines which she has taken over. That she should have taken such early action might perhaps be understood on the ground that the son of the German Under-Secretary of State, von Weizsäcker, is attached to the Kaiser-Wilhelm-Institute in Berlin where some of the American work on uranium is now being repeated.

Yours very truly,
Albert Einstein

Einstein read the letter with great care. He made only one comment: "This would be the first time that nuclear energy would be used directly instead of indirectly through the processes in the sun." That comment struck me, even before I had read the actual letter some years later, as a peculiar comment for the letter's author to make upon rereading it. The letter, no doubt, had resulted from conversations between Szilárd and Einstein, and probably between Szilárd and [physicist Eugene] Wigner. But of the three, I suspect only Szilárd would have felt so free as to instruct the president of the United States in detail about what to do. Einstein signed the letter, and we left.

Funding the Chain Reactor

I heard that Szilárd gave the letter to Alexander Sachs, a banker and an acquaintance of Roosevelt's, who promised to have it delivered to the president. That method of postal service proved slow but effective. Almost ten weeks later, a psychologically ideal moment occurred (after Hitler and Stalin had conquered and divided Poland), and the letter arrived. Roosevelt acted at once. The president set up an Advisory Committee on Uranium, and appointed D. Lyman Briggs, the head of the Bureau of Standards, its chairman.

Briggs called a meeting for October 21, and Sachs saw to it that Szilárd, Wigner, Fermi, and I were among those invited. But Fermi didn't want to attend, so I was again delegated to change his mind. On this occasion, however, Fermi could not be moved. His experience with asking for support from the navy had convinced him that he wanted nothing more to do with governmental meetings. "But," he told me, "I will tell you what I'd say if I were to go. You can deliver the message," Thus, I was promoted from chauffeur to messenger boy.

The army was represented at that meeting by a Colonel Keith F. Adamson from the Aberdeen Weapons Proving Grounds. After the initial presentation, Adamson began by voicing his doubts about novel scientific projects: "At Aberdeen, we're offering a $10,000 reward to anyone who can use a death ray to kill the goat we have tethered to a post. That goat is still perfectly healthy. Furthermore, weapons have far less to do with winning wars than does moral superiority." His comment might have been inspiring except that the recent victory in Poland belonged to Hitler and Stalin; I could not associate moral superiority with either of them.

Szilárd and Wigner continued to press the case for supporting research on fission, and after some time, I was called upon. After stating that I was merely transmitting Fermi's message, I explained that the first necessary project was to construct a chain reactor. The researchers at Columbia would volunteer their labor, I noted (on Fermi's instruction); but slowing neutrons without absorbing them requires a great amount of exceptionally pure graphite, and that would be expensive. "In fact," I added, "a sufficient amount of graphite would cost about $6,000." The committee promptly granted us $6,000. . .

Roosevelt's Speech

During that academic year, the fission research at Columbia developed slowly. I was uncertain whether I wanted to remain a bystander or become a participant. I was content and pleased with the way my small world was running. I was a professor, as I had dreamed of being. Yet, although I was happy in academia, the possibility of the new weapon made me worry.

In early May 1940, together with a few thousand other scientists, I was invited to attend a Pan American Congress at which President Roosevelt was to speak. I did not plan to attend. In my five years in Washington, I had never visited the Capitol or seen an important political figure. Then, two days before the meeting, the phony war turned into a fast-moving conquest. Using modern tanks and dive bombers to prepare the way, the Nazi armies swept triumphantly through Holland, Belgium, and Luxembourg. The Nazi Blitzkreig, the lightning-strike war, was terrifyingly effective. I decided to accept the invitation and hear the president.

President Roosevelt talked that day about inherent human rights and the blessings of democracy, and about the progress made through science and technology in conquering disease and poverty. Then he became more specific about the war:

> In modern terms, it is a shorter distance from Europe to San Francisco, California, than it was for the ships and the legions of Julius Caesar to move from home to Spain. . . .
>
> You who are scientists may have been told that you are in part responsible for the debacle of today because of the processes of invention for the annihilation of time and space, but I assure you it is not the scientists of the world who are responsible, because the objectives which you held have looked toward closer and more peaceful relations between all nations through the spirit of cooperation and the interchange of knowledge. . . .
>
> The great achievements of science and even of art can be used in one way or another, to destroy as well as create. They are only instruments by which men try to do the things they most want to do. . . .

Can we continue our peaceful construction if all other continents embrace by preference or by compulsion a wholly different principle of life? No, I think not.

Surely it is time . . . to use every knowledge, every science we possess, to apply common sense and above all to act with unanimity and singleness of purpose.

I am a pacifist. You, my fellow citizens of twenty-one American republics, are pacifists too.

But I believe that . . . you and I, if in the long run it be necessary, will act together to protect and defend by every means at our command, our science, our culture, our American freedom and our civilization.

Seated in the crowd of thousands that day, I had the peculiar feeling that the president was speaking directly to me. Perhaps that is what is meant by charisma. But I also suspected that, out of all those present, the president and I were probably the only people who associated "using every knowledge, every science we possess" with the race for the atomic bomb.

I remember that at the end of his speech, I looked at my watch. Roosevelt's speech had taken twenty minutes, and in that time, he had resolved my dilemma. I was one of the fortunate helped to escape from the Nazi threat. I was now enjoying the comforts and many benefits of living in a democracy. I had the obligation to do whatever I could to protect freedom.

The MAUD Report

The MAUD Committee

After the initial discovery of fission by European scientists, the key theoretical work on building the bomb was worked out in England in 1940 and 1941 by two refugee German physicists, Rudolf Peierls and Otto Frisch. Their work led to a secret report by a British government committee code-named the MAUD Committee. The 1941 report stated that a bomb could be constructed from twenty-five pounds of uranium that "would be equivalent as regards destructive effect to 1,800 tons of T.N.T." But making the bomb would be a very large and expensive operation. The report concluded that despite the cost of the enormous engineering and manufacturing operation needed to produce the bomb, "the destructive effect both material and moral, is so great that every effort should be made to produce bombs of this kind."

The report explains in very clear terms what fission is and how it is used to produce a nuclear bomb. It also examines the great damage that an atomic bomb would cause, including the release of radioactivity, "which would make places near to where the bomb exploded dangerous to human life for a long period." The MAUD report was sent to President Roosevelt and led to the funding of the Manhattan Project.

W ork to investigate the possibilities of utilising the atomic energy of uranium for military purposes has been in progress since 1939, and a stage has now been reached when it seems desirable to report progress.

We should like to emphasise at the beginning of this report that we entered the project with more scepticism than

Excerpted from "The MAUD Report, 1941," by The M.A.U.D. Committee on the Use of Uranium for a Bomb, *Britain and Atomic Energy, 1939–1945*, by Margaret Gowing (New York: St. Martin's Press, 1964). Copyright © 1964 by Palgrave Global Publishing at St. Martin's Press. Reprinted with permission.

belief, though we felt it was a matter which had to be investigated. As we proceeded we became more and more convinced that release of atomic energy on a large scale is possible and that conditions can be chosen which would make it a very powerful weapon of war. We have now reached the conclusion that it will be possible to make an effective uranium bomb which, containing some 25 lb of active material, would be equivalent as regards destructive effect to 1,800 tons of T.N.T. and would also release large quantities of radioactive substance, which would make places near to where the bomb exploded dangerous to human life for a long period. The bomb would be composed of an active constituent (referred to in what follows as ^{235}U) present to the extent of about a part in 140 in ordinary Uranium. Owing to the very small difference in properties (other than explosive) between this substance and the rest of the uranium, its extraction is a matter of great difficulty and a plant to produce 2¼ lb (1 kg) per day (or 3 bombs per month) is estimated to cost approximately £5,000,000, of which sum a considerable proportion would be spent on engineering, requiring labour of the same highly skilled character as is needed for making turbines.

In spite of this very large expenditure we consider that the destructive effect, both material and moral, is so great that every effort should be made to produce bombs of this kind. As regards the time required, Imperial Chemical Industries after consultation with Dr. Guy of Metropolitan-Vickers, estimate that the material for the first bomb could be ready by the end of 1943. This of course assumes that no major difficulty of an entirely unforeseen character arises. Dr. Ferguson of Woolwich estimates that the time required to work out the method of producing high velocities required for fusing . . . is 1–2 months. As this could be done concurrently with the production of the material no further delay is to be anticipated on this score. Even if the war should end before the bombs are ready the effort would not be wasted, except in the unlikely event of complete disarmament, since no nation would care to risk being caught without a weapon of such decisive possibilities.

We know that Germany has taken a great deal of trouble to secure supplies of the substance known as heavy water. In the earlier stages we thought that this substance might be of great importance for our work. It appears in fact that its usefulness in the release of atomic energy is limited to processes which are not likely to be of immediate war value, but the Germans may by now have realised this, and it may be mentioned that the lines on which we are now working are such as would be likely to suggest themselves to any capable physicist.

By far the largest supplies of uranium are in Canada and the Belgian Congo, and since it has been actively looked for because of the radium which accompanies it, it is unlikely that any considerable quantities exist which are unknown except possibly in unexplored regions.

Principle Involved

This type of bomb is possible because of the enormous store of energy resident in atoms and because of the special properties of the active constituent of uranium. The explosion is very different in its mechanism from the ordinary chemical explosion, for it can occur only if the quantity of ^{235}U is greater than a certain critical amount. Quantities of the material less than the critical amount are quite stable. Such quantities are therefore perfectly safe and this is a point which we wish to emphasise. On the other hand, if the amount of material exceeds the critical value it is unstable and a reaction will develop and multiply itself with enormous rapidity, resulting in an explosion of unprecedented violence. Thus all that is necessary to detonate the bomb is to bring together two pieces of the active material each less than the critical size but which when in contact form a mass exceeding it.

Method of Fusing

In order to achieve the greatest efficiency in an explosion of this type, it is necessary to bring the two halves together at high velocity and it is proposed to do this by firing them together with charges of ordinary explosive in a form of double gun.

The weight of this gun will of course greatly exceed the weight of the bomb itself, but should not be more than 1 ton,

The Impact of the MAUD Report

In 1940, America was not yet at war. President Roosevelt, aware of the destructive potential of an atomic bomb, had authorized more research into the bomb by setting up the Uranium Committee with a small budget of $50,000. Despite the warning of such scientists as Enrico Fermi, Edward Teller, and Leo Szilard, many American physicists were doubtful that the atomic bomb would be practical. The Uranium Committee proceeded cautiously and slowly. Meanwhile in Britain, Otto Frisch was working on the atom bomb with German physicist Rudolph Peierls. Frisch, who one year earlier coined the term "fission," had left Denmark in advance of the threatened Nazi invasion. The research done by Frisch and Peierls in Britain formed the basis of a report by a secret British committee code-named MAUD. In the following excerpt from his book The Manhattan Project, *Don E. Beyer discusses the impact of the MAUD Report upon the development of the atomic bomb.*

Thus, as America's friends struggled for survival in Europe and as events moved the United States closer to war, the program that sought to harness the energy of the atom inched along with little energy of its own. By late 1940, less than $50,000 had been allocated for bomb-related research. Efforts to explore the explosive potential of nuclear fission were still relegated to the back burner of the administrative stove. The events of 1941 changed that. The first stimulus came from Great Britain.

Fission research in Great Britain was also proceeding slowly because of significant doubts about the possibility of making bombs. The work of two emigré scientists, Otto Frisch and Rudolph Peierls, changed the minds of British policy makers and directly influenced American military priorities. When war broke out in Europe, Otto Frisch was in England visiting Mark Oliphant, head of the physics department at Birmingham, who was engaged in war-related work. Fearing that Denmark might soon fall to Hitler, Frisch

and it would certainly be within the carrying capacity of a modern bomber. It is suggested that the bomb (contained in

decided not to return to his position at the Bohr Institute in Copenhagen. He found important work to do in England. Collaborating with Peierls, a German physicist who had been in England since 1933, Frisch pursued the possibility of using fast neutrons for the fission of U-235, a naturally occurring isotope of uranium, at a time when American scientists were investigating the potential for fission by slow neutrons. Frisch and Peierls sought answers to several key questions: Was the fission of U-235 by fast neutrons actually possible? If so, how strong was this fission process? Could enough U-235 be separated from natural uranium to make it work in a bomb? How much would be needed?

The answers to these questions, worked out in the spring of 1941, formed the basis of a report by a British committee, code-named MAUD, organized to review the potential for atomic bomb development. The conclusions of the MAUD Report were bold and disturbing. It maintained that the development of an atomic bomb fueled by U-235 was not only possible but could be completed in a minimum of three years. Furthermore, the destructive potential of such a bomb was tremendous and was "likely to lead to decisive results in the war." Facilities to separate enough U-235 to fuel a production line of bombs could be constructed at an estimated cost of £5,000,000. In recommending "the highest priority" for a bomb project, even if the war should end before bombs were ready, the MAUD Report foresaw the significance of atomic weapons in the postwar future.

Though the MAUD Report was not officially released until October 1941, copies of a draft were in the hands of key American administrators several months earlier. . . . The weight of the British MAUD Report and urgent voices at home finally convinced key American scientists and administrators that the United States must commit to building the bomb. When an official copy of the MAUD Report reached President Roosevelt in October 1941, the president acted.

Don E Beyer, *The Manhattan Project*. New York: Franklin Watts, 1991.

the gun) should be dropped by parachute and the gun should be fired by means of a percussion device when it hits the ground. The time of drop can be made long enough to allow the aeroplane to escape from the danger zone, and as this is very large, great accuracy of aim is not required.

Probable Effect

The best estimate of the kind of damage likely to be produced by the explosion of 1,800 tons of T.N.T. is afforded by the great explosion at Halifax N.S. [Nova Scotia] in 1917. The following account is from the *History of Explosives*. "The ship contained 450,000 lb of T.N.T., 122,960 lb of guncotton, and 4,661,794 lb of picric acid wet and dry, making a total of 5,234,754 lb. The zone of the explosion extended for about ¾ mile in every direction and in this zone the destruction was almost complete. Severe structural damage extended generally for a radius of 1-⅛ to 1-¼ miles, and in one direction up to 1-¾ miles from the origin. Missiles were projected to 3–4 miles, window glass broken up to 10 miles generally, and in one instance up to 61 miles."

In considering this description it is to be remembered that part of the explosives cargo was situated below water level and part above.

Preparation of Material and Cost

We have considered in great detail the possible methods of extracting the ^{235}U from ordinary uranium and have made a number of experiments. The scheme which we recommend is described in Part II of this report and in greater detail in Appendix IV. It involves essentially the gaseous diffusion of a compound of uranium through gauzes of very fine mesh.

In the estimates of size and cost which accompany this report, we have only assumed types of gauze which are at present in existence. It is probable that a comparatively small amount of development would enable gauzes of smaller mesh to be made and this would allow the construction of a somewhat smaller and consequently cheaper separation plant for the same output.

Although the cost per lb of this explosive is so great it compares very favourably with ordinary explosives when reckoned in terms of energy released and damage done. It is, in fact considerably cheaper, but the points which we regard as of overwhelming importance are the concentrated destruction which it would produce, the large moral effect, and the saving in air effort the use of this substance would allow, as compared with bombing with ordinary explosives.

Discussion

One outstanding difficulty of the scheme is that the main principle cannot be tested on a small scale. Even to produce a bomb of the minimum critical size would involve a great expenditure of time and money. We are however convinced that the principle is correct, and whilst there is still some uncertainty as to the critical size it is most unlikely that the best estimate we can make is so far in error as to invalidate the general conclusions. We feel that the present evidence is sufficient to justify the scheme being strongly pressed.

As regards the manufacture of the ^{235}U we have gone nearly as far as we can on a laboratory scale. The principle of the method is certain, and the application does not appear unduly difficult as a piece of chemical engineering. The need to work on a larger scale is now very apparent and we are beginning to have difficulty in finding the necessary scientific personnel. Further, if the weapon is to be available in say two years from now, it is necessary to start plans for the erection of a factory, though no really large expenditure will be needed till the 20-stage model has been tested. It is also important to begin training men who can ultimately act as supervisors of the manufacture. There are a number of auxiliary pieces of apparatus to be developed, such as those for measuring the concentration of the ^{235}U. In addition, work on a fairly large scale is needed to develop the chemical side for the production in bulk of uranium hexafluoride, the gaseous compound we propose to use.

It will be seen from the foregoing that a stage in the work has now been reached at which it is important that a decision should be made as to whether the work is to be continued on the increasing scale which would be necessary if we are to hope for it as an effective weapon for this war. Any considerable delay now would retard by an equivalent amount the date by which the weapon could come into effect.

Action in the U.S.

We are informed that while the Americans are working on the uranium problem the bulk of their effort has been directed to the production of energy, as discussed in our report on uranium as a source of power, rather than to the production of a bomb. We are in fact co-operating with the United States to the extent of exchanging information, and they have undertaken one or two pieces of laboratory work for us. We feel that it is important and desirable that development work should proceed on both sides of the Atlantic irrespective of where it may be finally decided to locate the plant for separating the ^{235}U, and for this purpose it seems desirable that certain members of the committee should visit the United States. We are informed that such a visit would be welcomed by members of the United States committees which are dealing with this matter.

Conclusions and Recommendations

(i) The committee considers that the scheme for a uranium bomb is practicable and likely to lead to decisive results in the war.

(ii) It recommends that this work be continued on the highest priority and on the increasing scale necessary to obtain the weapon in the shortest possible time.

(iii) That the present collaboration with America should be continued and extended especially in the region of experimental work.

Chapter 2

The Manhattan Project

Chapter Preface

With the creation of the Manhattan Project in August 1942, the U.S. government had an organization that could manage the complex and costly effort needed to build the atomic bomb. However, the practicality of the bomb still had to be proven. The first big step toward making the bomb a reality was taken in Chicago in an unused squash court. Here Enrico Fermi and Leo Szilard built the first working atomic pile. The pile was made of alternating layers of uranium and graphite blocks stacked or piled into a cube. The graphite was needed within the pile to slow down the bombarding neutrons so they could be absorbed by the nucleus of the uranium atoms. The pile also contained control rods made of cadmium that prevented a chain reaction until they were removed. On December 2, 1942, Fermi gave the order to withdraw the control rods. Neutrons emitted by the uranium split other uranium atoms producing more neutrons and in turn splitting more uranium atoms. The chain reaction became self-sustaining by 3:30 that afternoon. Fermi's group had proved that a chain reaction could be achieved and that the bomb was a practical reality.

When Brigadier General Leslie Groves became the head of the Manhattan Project in September 1942, he quickly made several critical decisions toward organizing the work on the bomb. He immediately began construction of two huge refineries at Oakridge, Tennessee, and Hanford, Washington. These refineries would manufacture the fissionable fuel for the bomb. Oakridge would refine uranium 235 and Hanford would make plutonium. The process of making fuel for the bomb was extremely complex and slow. If these refineries had not been established early on, the bomb would never have been made before the war ended.

The other crucial decision Groves made was the establishment of Los Alamos Laboratory. On October 8, 1942, Groves met physicist J. Robert Oppenheimer at Berkeley, California. They discussed the research he was doing on the atomic bomb. As Groves wrote in a 1970 article, "Our discussion confirmed my previous belief that we should bring all of the widely scattered theoretical work together in one place. . . . He [Oppenheimer] expressed complete agreement, and it was then that the idea of the prompt establishment of a Los Alamos was conceived." Groves named Oppenheimer as the scientific head on the Manhattan Project shortly after their meeting in Berkeley. Oppenheimer recruited the best scientists in the United States and Britain to work on the design of the bomb at Los Alamos.

After two and a half years of feverish work, the effort at Los Alamos culminated with the Trinity Test—the explosion of the first plutonium nuclear bomb at Alamogordo, New Mexico, on July 16, 1945. The bomb was detonated at 5:30 A.M. As the official War Department report states, "There was a blinding flash lighting up the whole area brighter than the brightest daylight. . . . A huge multi-colored surging cloud boiled to an altitude of over 40,000 feet." The Trinity Test was a complete success and the Manhattan Project had proven that its huge expenditures had been fruitful.

Yet after Trinity, many felt a sense of horror, regret and even guilt at what they had accomplished. The fact that Germany had already been defeated left some scientists with second thoughts about building the bomb. As one Manhattan Project scientist, Robert R. Wilson, wrote about his reaction to witnessing the Trinity Test, "My technical work was done, the race was run and the full magnitude of what we had done came over me."

The First Chain Reaction

Corbin Allardice and Edward R. Trapnell

In 1942, a group of scientists headed by Enrico Fermi and Arthur Compton was building an atomic pile that they hoped would become the first nuclear reactor. This reactor consisted of a stack, or pile, of graphite blocks with lumps of uranium spaced throughout. The graphite served to slow down the neutrons emitted by the uranium so that they would be absorbed by the next lump of uranium and cause it to fission. It was hoped that this process would continue until the overall reaction became continuous and self-sustaining.

The atomic pile was built under the squash courts in the stadium of the University of Chicago. Movable rods of cadmium were inserted into the pile. These rods could absorb the uranium emissions and could speed up or shut down the reaction.

By December 1, everything was ready for the crucial test. As Fermi, Compton, and the other scientists gathered around the instruments, the question on everyone's mind: Would the pile produce a self-sustaining chain reaction? If the reaction did sustain itself, the scientists could be certain that their assumptions about subatomic processes were correct. They could then move on to controlling the release of energy and the manufacture of an atomic warhead. The following informative account of the testing of the nuclear pile was written by two eyewitnesses, Corbin Allardice and Edward R. Trapnell, and published by the United States Atomic Energy Commission in 1949.

Excerpted from *The First Atomic Pile: An Eye-Witness Account Revealed by Some of the Participants and Narratively Recorded*, by Corbin Allardice and Edward R. Trapnell (Washington, DC: The United States Atomic Energy Commission, 1949).

An outsider looking into the squash court where Fermi was working would have been greeted by a strange sight. In the center of the 30 by 60-foot room, shrouded on all but one side by a gray balloon-cloth envelope, was a pile of black bricks and wooden timbers, square at the bottom and a flattened sphere on top. Up to half of its height, its sides were straight. The top half was domed, like a beehive. During the construction of this crude-appearing but complex pile (the name which has since been applied to all such devices) the standing joke among the scientists working on it was: "If people could see what we're doing with a million and a half of their dollars, they'd think we are crazy. If they knew why we were doing it, they'd be sure we are.". . .

At Chicago during the early afternoon of December 1, tests indicated that critical size was rapidly being approached. At 4:00 P.M. [Walter] Zinn's group was relieved by the men working under [Herbert L.] Anderson. Shortly afterward the last layer of graphite and uranium bricks was placed on the pile. Zinn, who remained, and Anderson made several measurements of the activity within the pile. They were certain that when the control rods were withdrawn, the pile would become self-sustaining. Both had agreed, however, that should measurements indicate the reaction would become self-sustaining when the rods were withdrawn, they would not start the pile operating until Fermi and the rest of the group could be present. Consequently, the control rods were locked and further work was postponed until the following day.

That night the word was passed to the men who had worked on the pile that the trial run was due the next morning.

About 8:30 on the morning of Wednesday, December 2, the group began to assemble in the squash court.

At the north end of the squash court was a balcony about ten feet above the floor of the court. Fermi, Zinn, Anderson, and [Arthur] Compton were grouped around instruments at the east end of the balcony. The remainder of the observers crowded the little balcony. R.G. Noble, one of the young scientists who worked on the pile, put it this way: "The control cabinet was surrounded by the 'big wheels'; the 'little wheels' had to stand back."

Safety Precautions

On the floor of the squash court, just beneath the balcony, stood George Weil, whose duty it was to handle the final control rod. In the pile were three sets of control rods. One set was automatic and could be controlled from the balcony. Another was an emergency safety rod. Attached to one end of this rod was a rope running through the pile and weighted heavily on the opposite end. The rod was withdrawn from the pile and tied by another rope to the balcony. Hilberry was ready to cut this rope with an ax should something unexpected happen, or in case the automatic safety rods failed. The third rod, operated by Weil, was the one which actually held the reaction in check until withdrawn the proper distance.

Since this demonstration was new and different from anything ever done before, complete reliance was not placed on mechanically operated control rods. Therefore a "liquid-control squad," composed of Harold Lichtenberger, W. Nyter, and A.C. Graves, stood on a platform above the pile. They were prepared to flood the pile with cadmium-salt solution in case of mechanical failure of the control rods.

Each group rehearsed its part of the experiment.

At 9:45 Fermi ordered the electrically operated control rods withdrawn. The man at the controls threw the switch to withdraw them. A small motor whined. All eyes watched the lights which indicated the rods' position.

But quickly the balcony group turned to watch the counters, whose clicking stepped up after the rods were out. The indicators of these counters resembled the face of a clock, with "hands" to indicate neutron count. Nearby was a recorder, whose quivering pen traced the neutron activity within the pile.

Reaction Levels Off

Shortly after ten o'clock, Fermi ordered the emergency rod, called "Zip," pulled out and tied.

"Zip out," said Fermi. Zinn withdrew "Zip" by hand and tied it to the balcony rail. Weil stood ready by the "vernier" control rod which was marked to show the number of feet and inches, which remained within the pile.

At 10:37 Fermi, without taking his eyes off the instruments, said quietly: "Pull it to 13 feet, George." The counters clicked faster. The graph pen moved up. All the instruments were studied, and computations were made.

"This is not it," said Fermi. "The trace will go to this point and level off." He indicated a spot on the graph. In a few minutes the pen came to the indicated point and did not go above that point. Seven minutes later Fermi ordered the rod out another foot.

Again the counters stepped up their clicking, the graph pen edged upwards. But the clicking was irregular. Soon it leveled off, as did the thin line of the pen. The pile was not self-sustaining—yet.

At 11 o'clock, the rod came out another six inches; the result was the same: an increase in rate, followed by the leveling off.

Fifteen minutes later, the rod was farther withdrawn and at 11:25 was moved again. Each time the counters speeded up, the pen climbed a few points. Fermi predicted correctly every movement of the indicators. He knew the time was near. He wanted to check everything again. The automatic control rod was reinserted without waiting for its automatic feature to operate. The graph line took a drop, the counters slowed abruptly.

At 11:35, the automatic safety rod was withdrawn and set. The control rod was adjusted and "Zip" was withdrawn. Up went the counters, clicking, clicking, faster and faster. It was the clickety-click of a fast train over the rails. The graph pen started to climb. Tensely, the little group watched and waited, entranced by the climbing needle.

Whrrrump! As if by a thunderclap, the spell was broken. Every man froze—then breathed a sigh of relief when he realized the automatic rod had slammed home. The safety point at which the rod operated automatically had been set too low.

"I'm hungry," said Fermi. "Let's go to lunch."

Perhaps, like a great coach, Fermi knew when his men needed a "break."

It was a strange "between halves" respite. They got no pep talk. They talked about everything else but the "game." The redoubtable Fermi, who never says much, had even less to say. But he appeared supremely confident. His "team" was back on the squash court at 2:00 P.M. Twenty minutes later, the automatic rod was reset and Weil stood ready at the control rod.

The Reaction Is Self-Sustaining

"All right, George," called Fermi, and Weil moved the rod to a predetermined point. The spectators resumed their watching and waiting, watching the counters spin, watching the graph, waiting for the settling down, and computing the rate of rise of reaction from the indicators.

At 2:50 the control rod came out another foot. The counters nearly jammed, the pen headed off the graph paper. But this was not it. Counting ratios and the graph scale had to be changed.

"Move it six inches," said Fermi at 3:20. Again the change—but again the leveling off. Five minutes later, Fermi called: "Pull it out another foot."

Weil withdrew the rod.

"This is going to do it," Fermi said to Compton, standing at his side. "Now it will become self-sustaining. The trace will climb and continue to climb. It will not level off."

Fermi computed the rate of rise of the neutron counts over a minute period. He silently, grim-faced, ran through some calculations on his slide rule.

In about a minute he again computed the rate of rise. If the rate was constant and remained so, he would know the reaction was self-sustaining. His fingers operated the slide rule with lightning speed. Characteristically, he turned the rule over and jotted down some figures on its ivory back.

Three minutes later he again computed the rate of rise in neutron count. The group on the balcony had by now crowded in to get an eye on the instruments, those behind craning their necks to be sure they would know the very instant history was made. In the background could be heard William Overbeck calling out the neutron count over an annunciator system. Leona Marshall (the only girl present), Anderson, and William Sturm were recording the readings from the instruments. By this time the click of the counters was too fast for the human ear. The clickety-click was now a steady brrrrr. Fermi, unmoved, unruffled, continued his computations.

"I couldn't see the instruments," said Weil. "I had to watch Fermi every second, waiting for orders. His face was motionless. His eyes darted from one dial to another. His expression was so calm it was hard. But suddenly, his whole face broke into a broad smile."

Fermi closed his slide rule—

"The reaction is self-sustaining," he announced quietly, happily. "The curve is exponential."

The group tensely watched for twenty-eight minutes while the world's first nuclear chain reactor operated.

The upward movement of the pen was leaving a straight line. There was no change to indicate a leveling off. This was it.

"O.K., 'Zip' in," called Fermi to Zinn, who controlled that rod. The time was 3:53 P.M. Abruptly, the counters slowed down, the pen slid down across the paper. It was all over.

Man had initiated a self-sustaining nuclear reaction—and then stopped it. He had released the energy of the atom's nucleus and controlled that energy.

Celebration

Right after Fermi ordered the reaction stopped, the Hungarian-born theoretical physicist Eugene Wigner presented him with a bottle of Chianti wine. All through the experiment Wigner had kept this wine hidden behind his back.

Fermi uncorked the wine bottle and sent out for paper cups so all could drink. He poured a little wine in all the cups, and silently, solemnly, without toasts, the scientists raised the cups to their lips—the Canadian Zinn, the Hungarians Szilard and Wigner, the Italian Fermi, the Americans Compton, Anderson, Hilberry, and a score of others. They drank to success—and to the hope they were the first to succeed.

A small crew was left to straighten up, lock controls, and check all apparatus. As the group filed from the West Stands, one of the guards asked Zinn:

"What's going on, Doctor, something happen in there?"

The guard did not hear the message which Arthur Compton was giving James B. Conant at Harvard, by long distance telephone. Their code was not prearranged.

"The Italian navigator has landed in the New World," said Compton.

"How were the natives?" asked Conant.

"Very friendly."

Manufacturing Plutonium and Uranium-235

Arthur H. Compton

While scientists were developing the mechanism of the atomic bomb at Los Alamos, two large separating plants in Oak Ridge, Tennessee, and Hanford, Washington, were producing fuel for the bomb. The Oak Ridge facility, officially known as the Clinton Engineer Works, was built in 1942. It initially produced both uranium-235 and plutonium. (Later plutonium production was shifted to the Hanford plant.) Uranium-235 and plutonium are the fissionable materials used to make nuclear bombs. To obtain these two rare elements, however, they must be extracted from uranium. Uranium-235 was separated from uranium-238 (the common form found in nature) at Oak Ridge through three methods: magnetic separation, liquid thermal diffusion, and gaseous diffusion. A less complex chemical separation was used to extract plutonium. Once extracted, uranium-235 was the explosive element used in the bomb "Little Boy" that was dropped on Hiroshima. Plutonium was the agent for "Fat Man," the bomb dropped on Nagasaki.

Arthur H. Compton was a member of the scientific team responsible for supplying the government with uranium-235 and plutonium. In the following excerpt from his 1956 book *Atomic Quest: A Personal Narrative*, Compton recalls how Oak Ridge, Tennessee, was chosen as the site to build the first

Excerpted from *Atomic Quest: A Personal Narrative*, by Arthur H. Compton (New York: Oxford University Press, 1956). Copyright © 1956 by Oxford University Press. Reprinted with permission.

separation plants. According to Compton, nuclear research scientists and engineers from the Du Pont Company were brought together to facilitate production at Oak Ridge. At first, the scientists were wary of letting a chemical manufacturing company oversee such a new project. However, Brigadier General Leslie Groves, the military officer in charge of the Manhattan Project, helped bridge the gap between the nuclear scientists and the Du Pont engineers. As Compton notes, "Neither group could have brought the enterprise to a successful conclusion without the other, nor would this powerful team have come together without the timely catalytic action of Brigadier General Groves." With Groves's prodding, the research scientists headed by Enrico Fermi, Glenn Seaborg, and Eugene Wigner worked in coordination with the engineering team led by Roger Williams and Crawford H. Greenewalt. The partnership proved beneficial, and the Oak Ridge facilities produced the nuclear fuel needed for America's new, but still untested, atomic weapons.

On 17 September 1942, General Brehon Somervell told General [Leslie] Groves, 'you have another job.' He sent him to General William D. Styer, who gave Groves his first information about the atomic bomb project. He was given until 23 September to prepare to take over its direction.

In his first review of the situation, Groves realized that the project needed immediate strengthening in its industrial phases. The first task was to get [plutonium] production in hand. Conant was ready with his recommendations based on our California meeting. Within twenty-four hours Groves had made his own personal inspection of the Tennessee Valley area and had approved the selection of a site along the Clinch River. Steps were immediately initiated to take over the area of almost eighty square miles that became Oak Ridge. Here was established the headquarters of the Clinton Engineer Works, named for the neighboring old village of Clinton.

To me this was familiar ground. Throughout the previous

spring we had been on the lookout for a site suitable for our plutonium production plant. Essential requirements were ample electric power, a good supply of water for cooling, a rugged terrain that would prevent an explosion in one portion of the plant from causing widespread disaster, adequate transportation, available labor supply, a climate that would permit winter construction, and preferably remoteness from the seacoast to make enemy attack more difficult. The Tennessee Valley fitted all these conditions except, surprisingly enough, that just at this time, because of the heavy demands of the new electrical industries that had moved into the area, there was little more power available than that needed to meet existing requirements.

Thomas Moore, our chief engineer, Richard Doan, Director of the Metallurgical Laboratory, and Norman Hilberry, associate project director, had gone to Knoxville early in May 1942. A day or two later my wife and I appeared in Knoxville as if for a holiday at the Great Smoky Mountains. The others had already inspected several sites under guidance of officials of the Tennessee Valley Authority (TVA). I spent half a day with them going over the Clinch River territory. We then went up beside the Norris Dam and looked at the housing used by the TVA project [which had been building dams in the region to harness hydroelectric energy].

Mr. Gordon R. Clapp, then General Manager of TVA and now its Chairman, discussed our problem with us. He welcomed our proposed operation, but added the plea, 'We hope you won't make an industrial slum of the area.' Instead of an 'industrial slum,' Oak Ridge has grown to be an attractive community whose operations have contributed greatly to the Valley's economy.

When we compared the merits of the various sites we had examined, I was inclined to favor a location in the Indiana dunes close to the shore of Lake Michigan. This would have been nearer to the center of the nation's industrial operations and could thus have been developed more readily. Moore convinced me, however, that this area was too exposed and not large enough to permit the expansion that our production facilities would require. We accordingly reported to Washington that the Tennessee area was our choice. A month later, when the Army was assigned its responsibility, Colonels K.D. Nichols and J.C. Marshall inspected the sites again and confirmed our recommendation.

Construction Begins

Fortunately, the region that we had located was hilly and sparsely populated. When Groves visited the Tennessee area in September he found it possible to extend the boundaries of the area from the two or three square miles that Moore and I had originally envisaged to include nearly eighty square miles and still not enclose any major village. The terrain was ideal for the purpose.

The speed with which the construction went ahead at Oak Ridge was phenomenal. In December 1942 ground was broken for the administration building. During the following winter work started on the electromagnetic separation plant, the plutonium semi-works 'Clinton Laboratory,' and the residential areas. In June 1943 a steam power plant of a quarter million kilowatts was begun to supply the electricity for the plants that were being erected.

It was the following spring, April 1943, that my wife and I made our next visit to Knoxville. Our chief concern at this time was the matter of housing for the hundreds of families associated with our research project that would need to go from Chicago into what was now a raw construction area. We were shown plans of typical houses that were to be erected by the thousands; we were shown where the schools, the church, and the shopping centers were to be built; and we saw where the roads were being cut through the oak-covered ridge that was to become the first residential area. Thus armed with information, we returned to Chicago. There my wife began her job of 'selling' Oak Ridge to the wives of the men who would build and work at our new pilot plant.

During the following summer the excavations and the construction of the great new uranium works were begun. I recall in particular the large hole where the immense oval magnet was to be built for the magnetic separation of the uranium isotopes. As Ernest Lawrence was showing it to me he spoke of the magnet as the race track—and that is just what it looked like. The name was symbolic, for it was this plant that was to turn out the first really significant amount of fissionable materials. . . .

Du Pont Becomes a Partner

During the autumn of 1942, while the du Pont Company was getting set to build the plutonium production plant, its engineers made repeated visits to our Chicago laboratory. It fell to my lot to give them a general view of the entire atomic project and a brief description of how plutonium was to be manufactured in a nuclear reactor. The science of nuclear transformations was completely foreign to them. But they were capable engineers accustomed to rely on tangible evidence. They would hear Enrico Fermi, with his matter-of-fact, methodical, lucid explanation, describe the reactor itself and the progress toward its laboratory operation. Finally Tom Moore and perhaps Eugene Wigner would tell how a production plant might be made to work. The dream began to take on the substance of reality. And then you could see these men, experienced in making technological processes work, shake themselves, figuratively at least, as they would try to get their thinking straight. Possible? Yes. But what a long road to travel before a useful amount of plutonium could be hoped for!

They were not the only ones asking this question. The dominant tone of the advice from the British observers at this stage was that of skepticism. Within the President's General Staff also were those who were continually counseling that the entire undertaking should be discarded as a dream of visionary scientists.

At the time of these interviews the only plans for a production plant that were far enough along to place before the du Pont engineers were those of Moore's helium-cooled reactor. How much better it would be if water could be used for cooling purposes, was their comment. We would explain the difficulty that water absorbs so many neutrons. But, we added, if a sufficiently thin layer of cooling water is used, it might just be possible. Wigner had a group of theoretical men now studying this possibility. It was too soon to predict what they would find.

As soon, however, as du Pont agreed to undertake the production of plutonium they put into the project their fullest possible effort. The responsibility for producing plutonium was assigned to the Company's Explosives Department of which Mr. E.B. Yancey was general manager. Within this department a new division was created with the sole task of carrying through the company's responsibility regarding plutonium production. In charge of this division was placed Mr. Roger Williams, as assistant general manager. Mr. Crawford H. Greenewalt was appointed technical director of the division. The co-operation of this experienced industrial organization gave strength to our plutonium project in just the places where it was most needed. . . .

A Joint Responsibility

Securing the acceptance of the du Pont engineers by the research men at the Metallurgical Laboratory was a major achievement. . . . A few months before the suggestion of putting the production of plutonium in the hands of an industrial organization had caused a near rebellion in the Laboratory ranks. Though the research team had at that time reluctantly agreed in principle, there were still a number of recalcitrant members, including some of the most influential research leaders. They wanted the production to be carried out under the laboratory's direction. But General Groves's position that production must be the responsibility of an industrial company familiar with production problems was so firm that it was evident to the laboratory men that only by co-operation with du Pont could they hope to make progress. The du Pont management did everything in its power to make the partnership work. Greenewalt handled his contacts with the laboratory admirably. Thus, though it took some time for the new relationship to become acceptable to the last few of the Met Lab's scientists, from the first du Pont's presence added greatly to our progress.

If you have ever spent hours paddling a loaded canoe alone against a heavy wind and have then taken on a partner who plies his own skilled and strong paddle beside your own, you will appreciate what it meant to the Metallurgical Project to have du Pont come in as a partner. Progress became positive and confident.

By this time the lines of research carried out by the Metallurgical Project were becoming exceedingly varied and widespread. To keep the work co-ordinated and directed, the heads of major research groups came together every two weeks. Usually this was at Chicago. Later the meetings were held occasionally at Oak Ridge. At one session technical advances would be reported. At another session policy would be considered, new problems continually arising would be discussed, and assignments made for their study.

I find in the record, for example, the minutes of the Laboratory Council meeting of 28 December 1942. Crawford Greenewalt was introduced as du Pont's representative. He told of du Pont's plans. Ten days earlier the company had formally agreed to take on the design of the plutonium-producing reactor 'with considerable trepidation' but would do everything in its power to 'translate a process into a reality.' He explained further that du Pont was not taking over the development aspects of the enterprise. Rather, as he put it, 'the Company will be the handmaiden to the Metallurgical Laboratory.' The whole enterprise was to be a joint responsibility.

When Greenewalt had finished, I explained to the Council that du Pont and the Met Lab were responsible in parallel to General Groves to see that plutonium was produced. It was an auspicious start. . . .

The Water-Cooled Graphite Pile

Within five weeks from Fermi's demonstration of the chain reaction, Eugene Wigner, working with Dr. Gale Young and a small core of other talented physicists, chemists, and engineers, placed before the Metallurgical Project Council plans for a water-cooled production plant. The procedure they had followed was a bold one. They assumed to start with that the neutron multiplication factor k would be substantially larger in the final structure than had as yet been demonstrated in the laboratory. They based this assumption on improvements that they could foresee in the purity of the uranium and graphite. But with this larger value of k they could afford to introduce not only a thin layer of cooling water but also a protecting sheath of aluminum that would prevent the water from corroding the uranium metal that it must cool. Although the water and the aluminum would absorb neutrons, their calculations indicated that this absorption would not be so great as to prevent a chain reaction from occurring. Their design called for long aluminum tubes embedded in the graphite moderator. Within the tubes were to be placed cylindrical slugs of uranium coated with aluminum. The cooling water would flow through the tubes around the uranium slugs. After sufficient exposure to the neutrons in the pile, the slugs would be pushed through the tubes into a deep water vat that would protect the operators from the intense radioactivity. Thence the slugs would be transferred to a chemical plant where the plutonium would be extracted from the uranium.

After a careful review the Council gave this plan its approval and passed it on to du Pont with a strongly favorable recommendation. The du Pont engineers foresaw a number of technical difficulties, but the general plan fitted well with their idea as to how heat could best be removed from the uranium where the energy was released. Accordingly, they agreed to accept the Wigner plan as the basis for designing the production plant.

A Powerful Team

It was a joy to be working now with the nation's first team. The ability of the du Pont organization was shown by the way they quickly assessed the merit of a plan dealing with phenomena that a few months before had been entirely unfamiliar. In an absolute minimum of time they transformed the plans into working designs and proceeded with plant construction, town building, and recruiting of workmen.

Worthy teammates were the men in the laboratory. Nowhere could have been found research men who would have used experiment and theory more rapidly and effectively to give a reliable plan for a plutonium-producing reactor. For those of less training and originality it was a task that would have been impossible. No previous practice existed as a guide. Only partial checks to the calculations could be made by experiment. The predictions must be accurate, for time was too precious to permit errors.

The art of co-ordinating specialized skills was required to high degree in designing, building, and operating the production plant. In this art, as well as in their own engineering specialties, Roger Williams, G.M. Reed, and Crawford Greenewalt of du Pont were past masters. In the laboratory it was originality, technical knowledge, and skill in exploring the unknown that counted. It was here that Enrico Fermi, Glenn Seaborg, and Eugene Wigner were supreme. Neither group could have brought the enterprise to a successful conclusion without the other, nor would this powerful team have come together without the timely catalytic action of General Groves and Colonel Nichols.

Following the plutonium project as it developed in the hands of such men was for me like watching a seasoned team in a World Series game, playing to win. Every man knew his task and did it with resourcefulness, confidence, and skill.

Wigner's training was at the University of Budapest, from which came to us also Leo Szilard and Edward Teller. The high competence of these men reflects the quality of the education given by this remarkable Hungarian institution. . . .

Wigner had seen firsthand the action of the Nazis and was acquainted with those who had felt their tyranny. He knew the competence of the German scientists. He had high respect for German industrial strength. His concern for the safety of the free world was real indeed. It was very difficult at first, however, for Wigner to believe that anything good could come from co-operation with a great industrial organization such as du Pont. Such companies, he had been taught in Europe, were the tyrants of the American democracy. It was only because of his eagerness to see the atomic program through to success that he was willing to undertake to help du Pont with their work. The du Pont engineers, mostly men of practical rather than theoretical experience, were also inclined perhaps to be skeptical of the usefulness of anything Wigner and his research team would turn out. When, however, they studied Wigner's plan for the water-cooled pile, they were impressed. Competent men themselves, they recognized a good piece of work when they saw it. As the months went by the relations between the two groups became more and more cordial, until not only mutual confidence but a considerable degree of admiration developed. The fact is, however, that underneath there remained a state of tension that caused continual concern to those responsible for the success of the undertaking.

The Work at Los Alamos and Alamogordo

Leslie R. Groves

Once the theoretical work regarding chain reactions had been realized in the Chicago experiments, the Manhattan Project moved along to the stage of building and testing an atomic weapon. Brigadier General Leslie R. Groves was the military head of the entire Manhattan Project. Groves consulted with J. Robert Oppenheimer, a distinguished theoretical physicist working on the bomb, to decide the best means to further the project. The two men agreed that it would be best to bring all the theoretical work being done in various cities around the country together in one location. They chose Los Alamos, New Mexico, as the best site to build an expansive design and testing laboratory. Los Alamos proved the perfect location because it was in a remote area, away from large populations of people. This meant that the area could be well secured and the work kept secret. The site also provided the necessary room for the construction of housing, schools, hospitals, and laboratories—all the facilities that would be needed by the military personnel, scientists, and their families who congregated at Los Alamos.

In a short memoir, excerpted in the following selection, Brigadier General Groves discusses the planning of the Los Alamos complex as well as the choosing of nearby Alamogordo, New Mexico, as the site for the actual test firing of

Excerpted from "Some Recollections of July 16, 1945," by Leslie R. Groves, *Alamogordo Plus Twenty-Five Years*, edited by Richard S. Lewis and Jane Wilson with Eugene Rabinowitch (New York: The Viking Press, 1971). Copyright © 1970 by the Educational Foundation for Nuclear Science, Inc. Reprinted by permission of Penguin Putnam, Inc.

the first atomic bombs. Although Groves's recollections were written down in 1970, he provides numerous details of the New Mexico facilities and the types of concerns he—and other officials—had for the safety of the researchers, military personnel, and any neighboring civilians who would be living near the dangerous nuclear materials.

I first met J. Robert Oppenheimer on October 8, 1942, at Berkeley, California. There, we discussed the theoretical research studies he was engaged in with respect to the physics of the bomb. Our discussions confirmed my previous belief that we should bring all of the widely scattered theoretical work together in one place and that there would have to be considerable laboratory work if our theories were to be relied on. He expressed complete agreement, and it was then that the idea of the prompt establishment of a Los Alamos was conceived.

Such a laboratory was particularly essential if we were to carry out our hoped-for plan of no test firing before use against the enemy. This was essential, not only to save time, but also to save precious material. We were fearful, indeed almost certain, that our production rates for fissionable materials would be extremely small. It should be remembered that, at this time, we did not know whether the reactor theory was valid or not and we had no idea at all as to whether we could build the enormous and extremely complex facilities that would be necessary to produce and then separate the needed plutonium. The gaseous-diffusion plant was still in the dream stage and only the magnetic-separation process seemed to have reached a point where it could be counted on; and, even then, production would be far from ample.

Search for a Laboratory Site

The Military Policy Committee agreed with my views and I started the search for what later became the site of the Los Alamos Laboratory.

The Los Alamos Laboratory site was selected after a very

careful examination of the possible areas in which such a
laboratory could be located. Once I had decided that such
an installation was necessary, I concluded that it should be
located in the southwestern section of the United States. It
was a section I knew well, for I had lived for a number of
years in Southern California and Arizona, and had traveled
a great deal throughout the Southwest.

There were several reasons for my decision. First, once
away from the Coast, the area in general was sparsely populated. Second, the climate lent itself to year-around construction activities, as well as to outdoor testing of component parts, if that became necessary—as we thought it
would. And, third, satisfactory transportation facilities, air
and rail, were generally available.

It was most desirable, even essential, that the laboratory
site be not too difficult of access from other areas of the project, particularly Berkeley, Chicago, Oak Ridge, and Washington. For security reasons, it had to be well removed from
the Pacific Coast and its exact location such as to discour-
age access both in and out. For safety, as well as security, it
had to be far away from any populated areas.

I directed Major J.H. Dudley, who was from Colonel
Marshall's Manhattan District Office, to make a survey of
the southwestern section of the United States, with a view
to locating a site which would meet these requirements. I
told him I thought he would find the general Albuquerque
area the most likely but that I wanted him to search the entire Southwest. He found one site in eastern California
which at first seemed quite attractive, but this we discarded
primarily because of the obvious transportation difficulties.
Major Dudley then arrived at a definite conclusion, this time
in the Albuquerque area.

I flew out there and then drove out to the proposed site to
make a personal inspection. Robert Oppenheimer, Major J.
H. Dudley, Edwin M. McMillan, and, I believe, John H.
Williams met me and we looked at the selected site. This
was in Sandoval County, along the Jemez River. I disap-
proved of it as soon as I saw it, much to McMillan's delight.

There was not sufficient space for expansion, if that should prove necessary. It was quite populated for the New Mexico countryside and it would have involved the taking of a number of small Indian-owned or operated farms and

Los Alamos: America's Athenian World

When Brigadier General Groves took over the Manhattan Project he insisted that security be maintained through "compartmentalization." This meant that a person would know only enough to carry out his job. The scientists did not like this policy. They felt that a free exchange of ideas was necessary to solve the complex and interrelated problems of building the bomb. Los Alamos Laboratory was founded in part as a solution to this dilemma between secrecy and open sharing of knowledge. At Los Alamos all the scientists working on the bomb lived and worked together in an isolated location where security could be maintained, and yet they could still collaborate on the bomb's design.

Los Alamos from 1943 to 1945 was a very stimulating environment in which to work. Some of the world's greatest scientists resided there including seven Nobel Prize winners: Niels Bohr, Enrico Fermi, Victor F. Weisskopf, Emilio Segrè, Stanislaw M. Ulam, Edward Teller, I.I. Rabi, John von Neumann, and Hans A Bethe. Ferenc Morton Szasz, in this excerpt from his book, The Day the Sun Rose Twice, *describes the heady atmosphere at Los Alamos.*

From 1943 to 1945, the tiny community of Los Alamos, New Mexico formed an unreal world, part mountain resort and part military base. Locally it was often termed "the Magic Mountain" or "Shangri-La." Those who came to the town after World War II frequently wished that they could have worked there earlier. For those who shared in the experience, remarked physicist I.I. Rabi, "it was their great moment.". . .

The men and women at Los Alamos formed an international community that was engaged in a life-or-death strug-

possibly part of the Indian reservation. This would have entailed dealings with Secretary of the Interior Harold Ickes, not an easy man to deal with and possessed of enormous curiosity, and with untold others. It would also have attracted

---

gle to beat the Germans to the secret of atomic power. This goal gave the town its fierce intensity. In 1975, physicist Hans A. Bethe confessed that never, either before or after, had he worked as hard as he did during his years at Los Alamos. "It was one of the few times in my life," said another well-known physicist, "when I felt truly alive."

Oppenheimer recruited many of the top personnel himself. His job was made easier by the fact that the scientists knew they would be applying their talents for the benefit of their country. They also knew that if they succeeded, they would become a part of history. . . . After some initial hesitation, recruitment snowballed, and by 1944 virtually every American physicist of importance was involved in the project. Some, however, were drawn into the work more by fate than by enthusiasm. "I worked on the bomb," one physicist confessed later, "because everybody I knew was doing it.". . .

It is probably safe to say that never before in the history of the human race have so many brilliant minds been gathered together at one place. Visitors walking through the spacious Fuller Lodge at lunch might see four to five Nobel Prize winners dining at the same time. If they had been able to divine the future, they would have known that seven other men would also become Nobel laureates. A list of those who worked at Los Alamos from 1943 to 1945 reads like a page from *Who's Who* for the world of science. . . .

In his memoirs, Otto Frisch, a member of the British delegation to Los Alamos, noted that he always felt he could knock on any Los Alamos door and soon find himself in a stimulating conversation on poetry, science, art, or music. Never had there been a community like it before; never would there be so again. It was America's Athenian world.

Ferenc Morton Szasz, *The Day the Sun Rose Twice*. Albuquerque: University of New Mexico Press, 1984.

undue public attention not only locally, but probably nationally, and thus would have blown security to bits. At this time, there was no thought that we might later need to test the completed bomb, and hence I felt that our outdoor testing would not require an extraordinarily large area but that we might need a number of widely separated smaller areas. In general, I felt that we needed a more isolated spot, one where there would be an extremely limited displacement of people, particularly Indians.

Los Alamos Is Chosen

It was not yet noon, and I did not want to waste the rest of the day; so I asked Oppenheimer if he knew any other possible sites in the area that we could see on our way back to Albuquerque. He suggested that the Los Alamos School might be a possibility. We drove over there, stopping en route for our lunch, a cold sandwich in a very beautiful but very cold spot along the road.

As soon as I saw it, I realized that this site was ideal for us. Although it was an early winter day, it was sunny and the weather was pleasant. The boys were wearing shorts and seemed to enjoy being out of doors. The only disadvantage was the entrance road up the hill from Santa Fe, which had some very sharp hairpin turns. I examined these and concluded that they could be modified satisfactorily and without too much delay or expense.

The site had several outstanding advantages. In the first place, it had a water supply more than adequate for more than three times the number of people that anyone estimated would be necessary. It was not sufficient, as we all learned later to our sorrow, for the actual population that occupied the area in 1945. Electric power was available as was limited telephone service. There were also several buildings which could be used to house the initial nucleus of our personnel. Thus, we could start organizing the laboratory promptly, without waiting for construction. Necessary expansion of facilities could be carried on as the laboratory began to function. Oppenheimer told me that he had heard that the school was having a hard time because of the war, and that the owner would probably be very glad if the property was taken over by the government. Arrangements were made promptly and Los Alamos came to life.

Search for a Bomb Test Site

In the early days, we believed that a gun-type bomb would be entirely satisfactory for both uranium-235 and for plutonium, and we did not feel that any full-scale test would be necessary. Later, when we learned that the gun-type would not be suitable for plutonium, we began to realize that we might find it advisable to test the implosion-type bomb. Also, by this time we were more confident that the plutonium process would be feasible to produce a reasonable amount of material. As soon as a full-scale test—and it had to be full-scale—became likely, we began the search for a suitable testing ground. Again, the widest latitude was given to the searchers, Kenneth T. Bainbridge, Major W.A. Stevens, and Major Peer DeSilva, all Los Alamos personnel, who reported directly to Oppenheimer. My only advice to the latter was that the site should be as close to Los Alamos as populated areas would permit, and that Indian reservations had to be avoided.

When the searchers under Oppenheimer's general direction came up with the Alamogordo site, I approved it without hesitation for it seemed to meet all of the requirements. It was well isolated, as will be confirmed by all of the participants in the test. It was within a reasonable distance of Los Alamos but not so near as to cause comment and thus endanger security. The nearby areas were thinly populated. The site itself was on an unpopulated area of a military reservation so that no real problem in securing and occupying the site promptly and easily was anticipated. The typical weather conditions were above average from our standpoint and, we thought (erroneously, as it turned out), easily predictable.

Soon after the initial selection, I arranged with Major General U.G. Ent, the Army Air Force Commander in Colorado Springs who had jurisdiction over the Alamogordo reservation, for our use of the area we had selected. This was not difficult for, at my request, General Arnold had long since instructed him to give us the utmost cooperation in any of our undertakings.

The first requirement at Alamogordo was an adequate base camp. This involved the construction of a number of temporary buildings. Simultaneously came the construction of miles of roads and the installation of extensive wire communications, the erection of the tower on which the bomb was to be detonated, and the provision of installations for the actual test operations. These were all relatively simple matters and required no supervision as far as I was concerned. Both Oppenheimer and I had complete confidence in Bainbridge, the scientist in charge of the test, as well as in the engineer and military-police officers who worked with him. We felt that our role was to support them in any way that they needed, so this phase was left almost entirely in their hands. Events proved that our confidence was not misplaced. . . .

Preparations for the Test

Brigadier General Thomas F. Farrell had joined the Manhattan Project early in 1945, and one of the first responsibilities assigned him was that of relieving me of many of my detailed responsibilities for matters pertaining to the test of the bomb and its use in combat. He was of tremendous assistance to me and to the Project, not only because of his over-all competence but also because of his happy faculty for getting along with people. This latter attribute became particularly important as we neared the time when we would learn that we had succeeded or failed and nerves became more jumpy, owing both to this and to the years of high-tension effort that so many individuals had put into the project.

Safety was a serious problem, the safety of both our own people and those in the immediate and general areas. We did not know just how big the explosion would be or what its effects would be, and we had to guess at all of the possibilities and do our best to see that each one was adequately taken care of.

As to our own personnel, we had no doubt that the control dugout some five miles from the site of the tower would provide ample protection for the group and equipment to be stationed there. We were also certain that it would be safe to be out in the open at the base camp, about ten miles distant, except for possible eyesight damage. This we felt was not too great a hazard, provided all exposed persons followed the procedure we prescribed of not looking at the expected fireball except through smoked glasses. The requirement later adopted—that observers at the base camp lie down with their heads away from the explosion and their faces toward the ground, while covering their eyes with their hands—was an extra precaution. It was thought to be desirable just in case the explosive force should turn out to be much greater than we anticipated.

The hazard that I feared the most was that of radioactive fallout on the areas over which the radioactive cloud would pass. This had not been considered for too many months as it was only at the turn of the year that Joseph Hirschfelder had brought up the possibility that this might be a serious problem. I learned later that the possibility of this danger had been indicated in the British Maud report, but I had been unaware of the existence of this report. It was this fallout hazard that caused us to be fearful of exploding the bomb when rain was likely to bring down an excessive fallout over nearby areas. We also could not ignore the old tales that heavy battle cannonading had sometimes brought on rain, although we knew of no scientific basis for any such phenomenon. I have never believed in ignoring such tales no matter how unreasonable they seemed, for sometimes they are unexpectedly justified by events.

The immediate military requirements can be summed up: adequate security (1) to prevent nonproject personnel from being within the immediate area; (2) to prevent injury to project personnel; (3) to diminish the likelihood of nonproject personnel learning of the explosion (our best way to avoid this was to set the time of the explosion at an hour when most people in the general area would be asleep); (4) to provide for the protection of residents of adjacent areas from radioactive fallout; (5) to provide for the prompt evacuation of any areas where any such fallout occurred; (6) to prevent any national press reports that could possibly alert Japan. This last was essential if we were not to impair the military surprise which we hoped would bring about the quick end of the war.

The Trinity Test

United States War Department

> The following news release by the War Department on the
> testing of the atomic bomb on July 16, 1945, includes eyewit-
> ness testimony by Brigadier General Thomas F. Farrell and
> Brigadier General Leslie R. Groves. They and a group of
> renowned scientists witnessed the momentous event that ush-
> ered mankind into the Atomic Age. The Trinity Test—named
> after the test site—took place in the remote desert of the
> Alamogordo Air Base, 120 miles southeast of Albuquerque,
> New Mexico. No one knew if the years of work on the bomb
> would culminate in a successful explosion. Tensions were
> high. So was anticipation, as the detonation was delayed
> because of an unpredicted rainstorm. When the rain stopped
> and the bomb was readied, the scientists and military
> observers took their posts in the control center 17,000 yards
> from the tower that held the bomb. As the two-minute count-
> down to detonation began, the assembled staff was ordered to
> lie on the ground with their heads away from the blast. Then
> came "the burst of light of a brilliance beyond any compari-
> son." Pent-up tensions were released with shouts of congratu-
> lations. It was certain that such an awesome weapon would
> speed the end of World War II. But the spectators also under-
> stood that the future of warfare had been forever changed in
> that bright flash of light.

M ankind's successful transition to a new age, the
Atomic Age, was ushered in July 16, 1945, before the
eyes of a tense group of renowned scientists and military

From "New Mexico Test, July 16, 1945," released by United States War Department, 1945.

men gathered in the desertlands of New Mexico to witness the first end results of their $2,000,000,000 effort. Here in a remote section of the Alamogordo Air Base 120 miles southeast of Albuquerque the first man-made atomic explosion, the outstanding achievement of nuclear science, was achieved at 5:30 A.M. of that day. Darkening heavens, pouring forth rain and lightning immediately up to the zero hour, heightened the drama.

Mounted on a steel tower, a revolutionary weapon destined to change war as we know it, or which may even be the instrumentality to end all wars, was set off with an impact which signalized man's entrance into a new physical world. Success was greater than the most ambitious estimates. A small amount of matter, the product of a chain of huge specially constructed industrial plants, was made to release the energy of the universe locked up within the atom from the beginning of time. A fabulous achievement had been reached. Speculative theory, barely established in prewar laboratories, had been projected into practicality.

This phase of the Atomic Bomb Project, which is headed by Brigadier General Leslie R. Groves, was under the direction of Dr. J.R. Oppenheimer, theoretical physicist of the University of California. He is to be credited with achieving the implementation of atomic energy for military purposes.

Tension before the actual detonation was at a tremendous pitch. Failure was an ever-present possibility. Too great a success, envisioned by some of those present, might have meant an uncontrollable, unusable weapon.

Final Assembly of the Bomb

Final assembly of the atomic bomb began on the night of July 12 in an old ranch house. As various component assemblies arrived from distant points, tension among the scientists rose to an increasing pitch. Coolest of all was the man charged with the actual assembly of the vital core, Dr. R.F. Bacher, in normal times a professor at Cornell University.

The entire cost of the project, representing the erection of whole cities and radically new plants spread over many miles of countryside, plus unprecedented experimentation, was represented in the pilot bomb and its parts. Here was the focal point of the venture. No other country in the world had been capable of such an outlay in brains and technical effort.

The full significance of these closing moments before the final factual test was *not* lost on these men of science. They fully knew their position as pioneers into another age. They also knew that one false move would blast them and their entire effort into eternity. Before the assembly started a receipt for the vital matter was signed by Brigadier General Thomas F. Farrell, General Groves' deputy. This signalized the formal transfer of the irreplaceable material from the scientists to the Army.

During final preliminary assembly, a bad few minutes developed when the assembly of an important section of the bomb was delayed. The entire unit was machine-tooled to the finest measurement. The insertion was partially completed when it apparently wedged tightly and would go no farther. Dr. Bacher, however, was undismayed and reassured the group that time would solve the problem. In three minutes' time, Dr. Bacher's statement was verified and basic assembly was completed without further incident.

Specialty teams, comprised of the top men on specific phases of science, all of which were bound up in the whole, took over their specialized parts of the assembly. In each group was centralized months and even years of channelized endeavor.

On Saturday, July 14, the unit which was to determine the success or failure of the entire project was elevated to the top of the steel tower. All that day and the next, the job of preparation went on. In addition to the apparatus necessary to cause the detonation, complete instrumentation to determine the pulse beat and all reactions of the bomb was rigged on the tower.

Weather Delays

The ominous weather which had dogged the assembly of the bomb had a very sobering affect on the assembled experts whose work was accomplished amid lightning flashes and peals of thunder. The weather, unusual and upsetting, blocked out aerial observation of the test. It even held up the actual explosion scheduled at 4:00 A.M. for an hour and a half. For many months the approximate date and time had been set and had been one of the high-level secrets of the best kept secret of the entire war.

Nearest observation point was set up 10,000 yards south of the tower where in a timber and earth shelter the controls for the test were located. At a point 17,000 yards from the tower at a point which would give the best observation, the key figures in the atomic bomb project took their posts. These included General Groves, Dr. Vannevar Bush, head of the Office of Scientific Research and Development and Dr. James B. Conant, president of Harvard University.

Actual detonation was in charge of Dr. K.T. Bainbridge of Massachusetts Institute of Technology. He and Lieutenant Bush, in charge of the Military Police Detachment, were the last men to inspect the tower with its cosmic bomb.

At three o'clock in the morning the party moved forward to the control station. General Groves and Dr. Oppenheimer consulted with the weathermen. The decision was made to go ahead with the test despite the lack of assurance of favorable weather. The time was set for 5:30 A.M.

General Groves rejoined Dr. Conant and Dr. Bush, and just before the test time they joined the many scientists gathered at the Base Camp. Here all present were ordered to lie on the ground, face downward, heads away from the blast direction.

Tension reached a tremendous pitch in the control room as the deadline approached. The several observation points in the area were tied in to the control room by radio and with twenty minutes to go, Dr. S.K. Allison of Chicago University took over the radio net and made periodic time announcements.

The time signals, 'minus 20 minutes, minus fifteen minutes,' and on and on increased the tension to the breaking point as the group in the control room which included Dr.

Oppenheimer and General Farrell held their breaths, all praying with the intensity of the moment which will live forever with each man who was there. At 'minus 45 seconds,' robot mechanism took over and from that point on the whole great complicated mass of intricate mechanism was in operation without human control. Stationed at a reserve switch, however, was a soldier scientist ready to attempt to stop the explosion should the order be issued. The order never came.

A Blinding Flash

At the appointed time there was a blinding flash lighting up the whole area brighter than the brightest daylight. A mountain range three miles from the observation point stood out in bold relief. Then came a tremendous sustained roar and a heavy pressure wave which knocked down two men outside the control center. Immediately thereafter, a huge multicolored surging cloud boiled to an altitude of over 40,000 feet. Clouds in its path disappeared. Soon the shifting substratosphere winds dispersed the now grey mass.

The test was over, the project a success.

The steel tower had been entirely vaporized. Where the tower had stood, there was a huge sloping crater. Dazed but relieved at the success of their tests, the scientists promptly marshalled their forces to estimate the strength of America's new weapon. To examine the nature of the crater, specially equipped tanks were wheeled into the area, one of which carried Dr. Enrico Fermi, noted nuclear scientist. Answer to their findings rests in the destruction effected in Japan today in the first military use of the atomic bomb.

Had it not been for the desolated area where the test was held and for the cooperation of the press in the area, it is certain that the test itself would have attracted far-reaching attention. As it was, many people in that area are still discussing the effect of the smash. A significant aspect, recorded by the press, was the experience of a blind girl near Albuquerque many miles from the scene, who, when the flash of the test lighted the sky before the explosion could be heard, exclaimed, 'What was that?'

General Groves' Testimony

Interviews of General Groves and General Farrell give the following on-the-scene versions of the test. General Groves said: "My impressions of the night's high points follow: After about an hour's sleep I got up at 0100 and from that time on until about five I was with Dr. Oppenheimer constantly. Naturally he was tense, although his mind was working at its usual extraordinary efficiency. I attempted to shield him from the evident concern shown by many of his assistants who were disturbed by the uncertain weather conditions. By 0330 we decided that we could probably fire at 0530. By 0400 the rain had stopped but the sky was heavily overcast. Our decision became firmer as time went on.

"During most of these hours the two of us journeyed from the control house out into the darkness to look at the stars and to assure each other that the one or two visible stars were becoming brighter. At 0510 I left Dr. Oppenheimer and returned to the main observation point which was 17,000 yards from the point of explosion. In accordance with our orders I found all personnel not otherwise occupied massed on a bit of high ground.

"Two minutes before the scheduled firing time, all persons lay face down with their feet pointing towards the explosion. As the remaining time was called from the loud speaker from the 10,000-yard control station there was complete awesome silence. Dr. Conant said he had never imagined seconds could be so long. Most of the individuals in accordance with orders shielded their eyes in one way or another.

"First came the burst of light of a brilliance beyond any comparison. We all rolled over and looked through dark glasses at the ball of fire. About forty seconds later came the shock wave followed by the sound, neither of which seemed startling after our complete astonishment at the extraordinary lighting intensity.

"A massive cloud was formed which surged and billowed upward with tremendous power, reaching the substratosphere in about five minutes.

"Two supplementary explosions of minor effect other than the lighting occurred in the cloud shortly after the main explosion.

"The cloud traveled to a great height first in the form of a ball, then mushroomed, then changed into a long trailing chimney-shaped column and finally was sent in several directions by the variable winds at the different elevations.

"Dr. Conant reached over and we shook hands in mutual congratulations. Dr. Bush, who was on the other side of me, did likewise. The feeling of the entire assembly, even the uninitiated, was of profound awe. Drs. Conant and Bush and myself were struck by an even stronger feeling that the faith of those who had been responsible for the initiation and the carrying on of this Herculean project had been justified."

General Farrell's Impressions

General Farrell's impressions are: "The scene inside the shelter was dramatic beyond words. In and around the shelter were some twenty odd people concerned with last-minute arrangements. Included were Dr. Oppenheimer, the Director who had borne the great scientific burden of developing the weapon from the raw materials made in Tennessee and Washington, and a dozen of his key assistants, Dr. Kistiakowsky, Dr. Bainbridge, who supervised all the detailed arrangements for the test; the weather expert, and several others. Besides those, there were a handful of soldiers, two or three Army officers and one Naval officer. The shelter was filled with a great variety of instruments and radios.

"For some hectic two hours preceding the blast, General Groves stayed with the Director. Twenty minutes before the zero hour, General Groves left for his station at the base camp, first because it provided a better observation point and second, because of our rule that he and I must not be together in situations where there is an element of danger which existed at both points.

"Just after General Groves left, announcements began to be broadcast of the interval remaining before the blast to the other groups participating in and observing the test. As the time interval grew smaller and changed from minutes to seconds, the tension increased by leaps and bounds. Everyone in that room knew the awful potentialities of the thing that they thought was about to happen. The scientists felt that their figuring must be right and that the bomb had to go off but there was in everyone's mind a strong measure of doubt.

"We were reaching into the unknown and we did not know what might come of it. It can safely be said that most of those present were praying—and praying harder than they had ever prayed before. If the shot were successful, it was a justification of the several years of intensive effort of tens of thousands of people—statesmen, scientists, engineers, manufacturers, soldiers, and many others in every walk of life.

"In that brief instant in the remote New Mexico desert, the tremendous effort of the brains and brawn of all these people came suddenly and startlingly to the fullest fruition. Dr. Oppenheimer, on whom had rested a very heavy burden, grew tenser as the last seconds ticked off. He scarcely breathed. He held on to a post to steady himself. For the last few seconds, he stared directly ahead and then when the announcer shouted "Now!" and there came this tremendous burst of light followed shortly thereafter by the deep growling roar of the explosion, his face relaxed into an expression of tremendous relief. Several of the observers standing back of the shelter to watch the lighting effects were knocked flat by the blast.

The Impossible Accomplished

"The tension in the room let up and all started congratulating each other. Everyone sensed 'This is it!' No matter what might happen now all knew that the impossible scientific job had been done. Atomic fission would no longer be hidden in the cloisters of the theoretical physicists' dreams. It was almost full grown at birth. It was a great new force to be used for good or for evil. There was a feeling in that shelter that those concerned with its nativity should dedicate their lives to the mission that it would always be used for good and never for evil.

"Dr. Kistiakowsky threw his arms around Dr. Oppenheimer and embraced him with shouts of glee. Others were equally enthusiastic. All the pent-up emotions were released in those few minutes and all seemed to sense immediately that the explosion had far exceeded the most optimistic expectations and wildest hopes of the scientists. All seemed to feel that they had been present at the birth of a new age—The Age of Atomic Energy—and felt their profound responsibility to help in guiding into right channels the tremendous forces which had been unlocked for the first time in history.

"As to the present war, there was a feeling that no matter what else might happen, we now had the means to ensure its speedy conclusion and save thousands of American lives. As to the future, there had been brought into being something big and something new that would prove to be immeasurably more important than the discovery of electricity or any of the other great discoveries which have so affected our existence.

"The effects could well be called unprecedented, magnificent, beautiful, stupendous and terrifying. No man-made phenomenon of such tremendous power had ever occurred before. The lighting effects beggared description. The whole country was lighted by a searing light with the intensity many times that of the midday sun. It was golden, purple, violet, gray and blue. It lighted every peak, crevasse and ridge of the nearby mountain range with a clarity and beauty that cannot be described but must be seen to be imagined. It was that beauty the great poets dream about but describe most poorly and inadequately. Thirty seconds after, the explosion came first, the air blast pressing hard against the people and things, to be followed almost immediately by the strong, sustained, awesome roar which warned of doomsday and made us feel that we puny things were blasphemous to dare tamper with the forces heretofore reserved to the Almighty. Words are inadequate tools for the job of acquainting those not present with the physical, mental and psychological effects. It had to be witnessed to be realized."

The Conscience of a Physicist

Robert R. Wilson

Early in his career as a scientist, Robert R. Wilson declared that all wars are evil and that he would not do research for any "futile, immoral war." But news of Nazi horrors coupled with his own scientific curiosity led Wilson to amend his moral stance in the initial years of World War II. Being a nuclear physicist, he became intrigued with fission. He learned that the work in fission was being directed toward the construction of an atomic weapon. With reservations, Wilson joined the Manhattan Project, but convinced himself that he would eventually use his discoveries in helping develop energy sources that would prove beneficial to humanity. Wilson invented a method of separating the rare uranium-235 isotope from the more commonly occurring uranium-238. Separating out uranium-235 was very important in making the atomic bomb. As his work continued, Wilson eased his conscience with the fact that he was helping to stop Adolf Hitler and the war in Europe.

Wilson then became the head of experimental research on the atomic bomb at Los Alamos, New Mexico, from 1944 to 1946. His team worked at a frantic pace so that the bomb would be ready as soon as possible. In the midst of the intense work on the Manhattan Project, Wilson did not question the morality of what he was doing. He was totally focused on making the project a success. After the bomb was built, tested, and dropped over Hiroshima, Wilson's conscience reasserted itself. He realized what destruction and suffering his work had

Excerpted from "The Conscience of a Physicist," by Robert R. Wilson, *Alamogordo Plus Twenty-Five Years*, edited by Richard S. Lewis and Jane Wilson with Eugene Rabinowitch (New York: The Viking Press, 1971). Copyright © 1970 by the Educational Foundation for Nuclear Science, Inc. Reprinted by permission of Penguin Putnam, Inc.

> caused. He again renounced working on weapons and decided
> to concentrate on deriving benefits from atomic power and to
> "go all out in helping to make it become a positive factor for
> humanity." In this reflective essay written in 1970, Wilson
> gives a penetrating portrait of a scientist wrestling with his
> conscience and the dangers of new technology.

[I]n the early 1940s], two graduate students from the Radiation Laboratory of the University of California at Berkeley were drinking coffee at the Student Union. Their conversation turned from nuclear physics, their usual obsession, to the war just breaking out in Europe. Very likely the left-wing discussion groups they had attended, or the anti-war demonstrations at Sather Gate, where they pushed their way at lunchtime, had an effect. They both agreed that the war in Europe was evil, that it would serve only to enrich the munition makers—the "Merchants of Death." They agreed that whatever might happen, and however justified the cause against Hitler might seem, the true course would be that of pacifism. They concluded with a friendly pact that come what may they would keep the faith, they would not get sucked into a futile, immoral war.

Working on Radar

A scant year later, the two young men confronted each other at a different radiation laboratory. This one was just being formed at the Massachusetts Institute of Technology to develop the electronic device that would soon become known as military radar. Remembering that pact of a year earlier, they looked at each other sheepishly and simultaneously asked, "But what are you doing here?"

I was one of the young men and a good deal had happened to me in the intervening year. I had gone on to Princeton University as an instructor, and there I had been exposed to a completely different climate of opinion. At Berkeley, sentiment had not differed greatly from the more virulent isolationism of the Midwest. Princeton, however, was a bastion of British sympathy. Some members of the physics department who had come from Britain were beginning to return for active duty. Refugee members, with a direct experience of Nazism, were exploring methods of becoming directly involved with the war; indeed, one of the most notable of the faculty tried to enlist in the Army in order to carry a rifle. He was rejected. In this hostile atmosphere, I pressed my quasi-isolationist, quasi-religious, and, believe me, unpopular point of view. I made no converts. Meanwhile, as Nazi might proved more and more successful, I grew more and more uneasy. If Hitler indeed conquered the world, could I bear to stand by and watch it happen, could I bear to think what life might be like?

In a matter of months, I received a telegram from my professor at Berkeley, Ernest Lawrence. He had sent similar telegrams to other former students, requesting that we appear in Boston for an emergency meeting. I went. There a team of British scientists dramatically described the Battle of Britain. They told us how they had helped in the battle by using radio waves to sense enemy airplanes. Lawrence and other senior scientists were proposing the formation of a laboratory at MIT to put a major effort into supplementing what the British were doing. I was asked to become a member of the laboratory.

That night I did not sleep. The alternatives seemed frightening. (I might add that thirty years later they still seem so.) It is one thing to take a philosophical position, such as pacifism, when only thoughts and statements, but not actions, are influenced. But it seemed to me that if ever the forces of darkness could be said to be lined up against the forces of light, it was at that time. There was no doubt that radar had already helped to win the Battle of Britain and that it would continue to play an important part in decisive air battles yet to come. Hence a technical person really could anticipate having a finite effect on the outcome of the war. That night, I chose against the purity of my immortal soul and in favor of a livable world. Rightly or wrongly, my conscience at the ready, I joined the new laboratory in the morning.

New Source of Energy—Fission

One dilemma of conscience resolved, another awaited me. When I returned to Princeton to make arrangements for my replacement as a teacher, Harry Smyth and Eugene Wigner drew me into a serious conversation. They described the studies, also just starting, at Columbia University concerning the application of the newly discovered fission of the nucleus to the development of a nuclear chain reactor. At that time, the end in view was not to be a bomb, but rather a new, and exceedingly intense, source of energy. Inasmuch as it was expected that the war would be a long one, such a powerful form of energy might be anticipated to have a serious, if not decisive, effect on the outcome. Smyth was persuasive in arguing that I, as a nuclear physicist, would be much more effective working with the cyclotron at Princeton on this new project than I ever could be working at MIT on a problem that was fundamentally electrical engineering. Well, in for a penny, in for a pound; I decided to work on nuclear energy.

I must confess that my decision to stay at Princeton was in some measure swayed by the consideration that I would be working on a basic source of energy that (I hoped) would become beneficial to everyone. At MIT, on the other hand, I would be involved directly in a nasty war, even though radar could then be construed as being wholly defensive. More thought about this, however, soon convinced me, perhaps wrongly, that any participation in war, offensive or defensive, served the same end, and that one could not distinguish between these two courses of action on moral grounds. Thirty years later, I have changed even that opinion. Obviously, there are differences in degree between an over-enthusiastic involvement in war and a lesser involvement that serves to protect family and friends.

Inventing the Isotron

The project at Princeton was moved to Chicago soon after Pearl Harbor. Just before that move, I learned of British measurements that indicated that a nuclear bomb could actually be built if a small quantity of U-235 could be separated from the more prevalent U-238. To my astonishment and horror, I invented a method (the isotron) of doing just that, and I was convinced that it would produce enough U-235 to make a bomb in about a year. Events in Europe had been going from bad to worse. Given the possibility that if we could produce a nuclear bomb, then the Germans could also produce one, it was not difficult for me then to take that next and most awful step. Thinking back to that time, it occurs to me that it would have been an excellent occasion for the conscience of a scientist to have been exercised. The idea of the isotope separator came to me in a flash of inspiration. But, at the same time, I fully realized the consequences of the idea were it to be successful. At just that moment of creation, I might have said to myself, "This is diabolical. To hell with it." Instead, I saw the isotron as a factor in reversing the tide of defeat and in stopping the carnage in Europe. I might just as well have spared myself that rationalization. New measurements showed that the early British measurements were wrong and that a bomb would actually require much greater amounts of U-235 than my method could possibly provide. Although I gave everything I had to the project at Princeton that was set up to develop the isotron, nevertheless I did not regret it when the project lost out in competition with other devices. Somehow, I felt that this failure relieved me (and my conscience) of a direct responsibility for a major contribution to the nuclear bomb. (Even so, my conscience still gives me an occasional twinge.)

Moving to Los Alamos

With the closing of the Princeton project, my colleagues and I, by now hardened soldiers, moved *en masse* to Los Alamos to help with the development of methods for the assembly of a bomb from fissionable materials being made elsewhere. At Los Alamos, we worked frantically so that a weapon would be ready at the earliest moment. Once caught up in such a mass effort, one does not debate at every moment,

Hamlet-fashion, its moral basis. The speed and interest of the technical developments, the fascinating interplay of brilliant personalities, the rapidly changing world situation outside our gates—all this worked only to involve us more deeply, more completely in what appeared to be an unquestionably good cause. . .

Impact of the Gadget

Something like a year after Los Alamos had started, I called a meeting in the cyclotron laboratory (Building X), which was under my direction. I remember placing notices around Los Alamos that announced a seminar sententiously entitled "The Impact of the Gadget on Civilization." I am hazy now as to who came or just what was said, but my impression is that a large part of the "intellectual contingent" turned out, including Oppenheimer. Our rather small meeting room was completely filled. We were by then, I think, aware that the Germans probably would not be able to make a bomb, and that the Allies were almost certainly going to win the war. We also knew that the United Nations Organization was about to be established—the conference which was about to take place at Dumbarton Oaks was very much on our minds. The thought most expressed at our discussion was that the United Nations could be set up on a proper basis only in the knowledge of the reality of nuclear weapons; that the only way this reality could become manifest would be by actually exploding a bomb; that our responsibility for a stable peace required that we work as hard as possible to demonstrate a bomb before the opening of the charter meeting scheduled to be held in San Francisco in April of 1945. (We missed that date. Did our failure have any effect on the organization of the United Nations? Would it have been organized differently had we already exploded a bomb? I doubt it.) At that time, we were perhaps overly obsessed by what we regarded as the evil of military security. We feared that the military would keep nuclear energy a secret were the bomb not revealed by an actual explosion. It is significant that no one at that meeting in Building X even raised the possibility that what we were doing might be morally wrong. No one suggested that we should pack our bags and leave. Instead, with missionary zeal, we resumed our work.

I have often wondered why it was that the defeat of Germany in 1945 did not cause me to re-examine my involvement with the war and with nuclear bombs in particular. The thought never occurred to me. Nor, to my knowledge, did any of my friends raise any such question on that occasion. Surely, it seems that among those hundreds of scientists at Los Alamos it might have been expected that at least one would have left. I regret now that I did not do so. It wasn't, I think, because of the rationalization concerning the United Nations. Perhaps events were moving just too incredibly fast. We were at the climax of the project—just on the verge of exploding the test bomb in the desert. Every faculty, every thought, every effort was directed toward making that a success. I think that to have asked us to pull back at that moment would have been as unrealistic and unfair as it would be to ask a pugilist to sense intellectually the exact moment his opponent has weakened to the point where eventually he will lose, and then to have the responsibility of stopping the fight just at that point. Things and events were happening on a scale of weeks: the death of Roosevelt, the fall of Germany, the 100-ton TNT test of May 7, the bomb test of July 16, each seemed to follow on the heels of the other. A person cannot react that fast. Then too, there was an absolutely Faustian fascination about whether the bomb would really work.

Coping with the Reality

I learned that a decision was in the process of being made concerning the first use of the bomb, probably some time in July. I argued that Japanese scientists should be invited to observe a test demonstration. But pushing such a view was almost impossible because my duties at that time were in the desert where the test was about to be made. Still I had confidence that my point of view would be expressed somewhere by someone, and I also felt confident that such a decision would be in good hands. I was horrified (but not surprised) when, on August 6, the bomb was exploded in anger over Hiroshima.

My reawakening from being completely technically oriented came dramatically on July 16 as I experienced the test explosion of the first nuclear bomb. It literally dwarfed the great desert basin of the Jornado del Muerto and the mountains all around it. That which had been an intellectual reality to me for some three years had suddenly become a factual, an existential reality. There is a very great difference. My technical work was done, the race was run, and the full awful magnitude of what we had done came over me. I determined at that moment that, having played even a small role in bringing it about, I would go all out in helping to make it become a positive factor for humanity. In this sentiment, I was by no means alone. Except for those scientists who were off to the Orient to help deliver a bomb, nearly everyone at Los Alamos began to consider intensely what could be done about the bomb. We wrote manifestos, we gave speeches, we made forays to Washington, we organized the Association of Los Alamos Scientists. Politics became our new business. When we learned of similar organizations at other laboratories, we amalgamated into the Federation of American Scientists. Part of the explanation of that eruption of idealism and activity, I believe, had to do with conscience unleashed after years of wartime suppression.

Conscience at Work

As soon as possible, I returned to university life, renouncing anything further to do with weapons work or, in fact, with any kind of work connected with secrecy. But even that kind of holier-than-thou course of action has since caused me considerable qualms. It was a kind of cop-out that is all too manifest in our youth today: good for my conscience, perhaps, but it immediately reduced my effectiveness to do something about nuclear energy. My expertise soon became outdated: I had to watch my more conservative friends, usually working from within the government, give the kind of advice and exert the kind of political pressure that is based upon understanding.

It seems to me that the efforts of scientists, of the kind generally characterized by what the Federation of American Scientists (FAS) does, have been remarkably effective in bringing about conditions under which we may even be able to survive nuclear energy. Their campaign to bring about a general understanding of the atomic bomb has been reasonably successful. (It was our great initial fear that no one would face up to that danger and, indeed, at first, no one did.) The efforts of scientists led directly to civilian control of nuclear energy. It could have been otherwise; the May-Johnson bill, intended to place nuclear energy in the hands of the military, might have become law instead of the McMahon bill. The vigorous response of the young scientists to the tocsin of "civilian control" dramatically blocked the May-Johnson bill and made possible the Atomic Energy Act of 1946 leading to the civilian Atomic Energy Commission. Similar efforts led eventually to the National Science Foundation. Scientists injected the issue of radioactive fallout into the election of 1956 and they kept after that issue until the test-ban agreement was consummated. But on the major issues, involving genuine disarmament, things have gone from bad to worse. Scientists themselves have been divided and, depending on their political beliefs, have perhaps contributed to the arms race more than they have tempered it—and, in every case, no doubt, strictly according to the dictates of conscience.

In spite of this, it appears to me that scientists have generally been pretty well motivated, that one can discern, dimly at times, conscience at work. How can the phenomenon of those eager young scientists of the first years of the FAS, frantically and effectively paying a political debt to society, be ascribed to anything but conscience?

Chapter 3

Using the Bomb

Chapter Preface

In 1945, Hitler's Germany was defeated. The question that now faced President Truman was should the United States use the atomic bomb against Japan. Truman had several committees of experts advising him on how to use the bomb. Two of these committees were the Interim Committee, mainly composed of top administration officials, and the Manhattan Project's Target Committee. The Target Committee was headed by Brigadier General Leslie Groves. It met in Robert Oppenheimer's office at Los Alamos in May 1945 and selected four Japanese cities as targets for the bomb: Hiroshima, Kokura, Yokohama, and Kyoto. Kyoto was later ruled out because it was an ancient cultural center. On June 1, 1945, the Interim Committee, headed by Secretary of War Stimson, "recommended that the bomb should be used against Japan, without specific warning, as soon as possible, and against such a target as to make clear its devastating strength."

Some scientists in the Manhattan Project did not agree with the conclusions of these two committees. One group of physicists, including Leo Szilard, Eugene Rabinowitch, Glen Seaborg, and James Franck, worried that dropping the bomb on Japan would lead to an arms race with Russia. In a report to Secretary Stimson, they proposed that, "a demonstration of the new weapon might best be made, before the eyes of representatives of all the United Nations, on the desert or a barren island."

President Truman had the final responsibility in making the decision to use the bomb. Truman did give Japan a warning at the Potsdam Conference in 1945. Truman in conjunction with Great Britain and Russia issued an ultimatum to Japan to surrender or be utterly destroyed. He did not, however, reveal the great power of the new weapon that the

United States now possessed. When Japan refused the ultimatum to surrender, Truman signed the orders that sent Paul Tibbets and his B-29 bomber crew on their mission, and on August 6, 1945, the "Little Boy" atomic bomb was detonated over Hiroshima.

Truman had no regrets about his decision. He was convinced that while the atomic bomb was a truly horrendous weapon, in the long run its use would save the United States from invading Japan with conventional forces and thus would save hundreds of thousands of American and Japanese lives.

Scientists Caution Against Using the Bomb

Committee on Political and Social Problems

The Franck Report, written by a committee of scientists—
including James Franck (serving as chairman) and Leo
Szilard—who had worked on the Manhattan Project, was submitted to Secretary of War Henry Stimson in June 1945. By
then Germany had been defeated, but Japan had not surrendered. The report addressed the question of whether America
should use the nuclear bombs against Japan in order to hasten
the war's end. Knowing the destructive power of the bomb
and the thousands of Japanese casualties that would result,
the committee's report argued for a demonstration of the new
weapon on a desert island rather than deploying it directly
against the enemy. The report predicted that if the bomb was
used militarily, it would set off an arms race and other nations
would acquire nuclear weapons, leaving the United States
vulnerable to future nuclear attack. The committee of scientists felt that America should not be the first nation to use
atomic weapons as a means of war. Instead, the United States
should organize an international campaign to prevent the
widespread proliferation of nuclear materials. In this way,
America would retain its image as a peacekeeping nation and
not be perceived as adding to world tensions.

While the Franck Report represented the views of some
scientists working on the bomb, it cannot be said to be the

Excerpted from *Report of the Committee on Political and Social Problems, Manhattan
Project "Metallurgical Laboratory,"* by J. Franck et al. (Washington, DC: U.S. National
Archives, 1945).

> official view of all those working on the Manhattan Project.
> There were many scientists, such as Enrico Fermi and J.
> Robert Oppenheimer, who supported a surprise attack on
> Japan as the best way to quickly end the war and save hun-
> dreds of thousands of American and Japanese lives.

Scientists have often before been accused of providing new weapons for the mutual destruction of nations, instead of improving their well-being. It is undoubtedly true that the discovery of flying, for example, has so far brought much more misery than enjoyment and profit to humanity. However, in the past, scientists could disclaim direct responsibility for the use to which mankind had put their disinterested discoveries. We feel compelled to take a more active stand now because the success which we have achieved in the development of nuclear power is fraught with infinitely greater dangers than were all the inventions of the past. All of us, familiar with the present state of nucleonics, live with the vision before our eyes of sudden destruction visited on our own country, of a Pearl Harbor disaster repeated in thousand-fold magnification in every one of our major cities.

In the past, science has often been able to provide also new methods of protection against new weapons of aggression it made possible, but it cannot promise such efficient protection against the destructive use of nuclear power. This protection can come only from the political organization of the world. Among all the arguments calling for an efficient international organization for peace, the existence of nuclear weapons is the most compelling one. In the absence of an international authority which would make all resort to force in international conflicts impossible, nations could still be diverted from a path which must lead to total mutual destruction, by a specific international agreement barring a nuclear armaments race.

Prospects of Armaments Race

It could be suggested that the danger of destruction by nuclear weapons can be avoided—at least as far as this country is concerned—either by keeping our discoveries secret for an indefinite time, or else by developing our nuclear armaments at such a pace that no other nations would think of attacking us from fear of overwhelming retaliation.

The answer to the first suggestion is that although we undoubtedly are at present ahead of the rest of the world in this field, the fundamental facts of nuclear power are a subject of common knowledge. British scientists know as much as we do about the basic wartime progress of nucleonics—if not of the specific processes used in our engineering developments—and the role which French nuclear physicists have played in the pre-war development of this field, plus their occasional contact with our Projects, will enable them to catch up rapidly, at least as far as basic scientific discoveries are concerned. German scientists, in whose discoveries the whole development of this field originated, apparently did not develop it during the war to the same extent to which this has been done in America: but to the last day of the European war, we were living in constant apprehension as to their possible achievements. The certainty that German scientists were working on this weapon and that their government would certainly have no scruples against using it when available, was the main motivation of the initiative which American scientists took in urging the development of nuclear power for military purposes on a large scale in this country. In Russia, too, the basic facts and implications of nuclear power were well understood in 1940, and the experience of Russian scientists in nuclear research is entirely sufficient to enable them to retrace our steps within a few years, even if we should make every attempt to conceal them. Even if we can retain our leadership in basic knowledge of nucleonics for a certain time by maintaining secrecy as to all results achieved on this and associated Projects, it would be foolish to hope that this can protect us for more than a few years. . . .

Our Greater Industrial Strength

We now consider the second of the two suggestions made at the beginning of this section, and ask whether we could not feel ourselves safe in a race of nuclear armaments by virtue of our greater industrial potential, including greater diffusion of scientific and technical knowledge, greater volume and efficiency of our skilled labor crops, and greater experience of our management—all the factors whose importance has been so strikingly demonstrated in the conversion of this country into an arsenal of the Allied Nations in the present war. The answer is that all that these advantages can give us is the accumulation of a larger number of bigger and better atomic bombs.

However, such a quantitative advantage in reserves of bottled destructive power will not make us safe from sudden attack. Just because a potential enemy will be afraid of being "outnumbered and outgunned," the temptation for him may be overwhelming to attempt a sudden unprovoked blow—particularly if he should suspect us of harboring aggressive intentions against his security or his sphere of influence. In no other type of warfare does the advantage lie so heavily with the aggressor. He can place his "infernal machines" in advance in all our major cities and explode them simultaneously, thus destroying a major part of our industry and a large part of our population, aggregated in densely populated metropolitan districts. Our possibilities of retaliation—even if retaliation should be considered adequate compensation for the loss of millions of lives and destruction of our largest cities—will be greatly handicapped because we must rely on aerial transportation of the bombs, and also because we may have to deal with an enemy whose industry and population are dispersed over a large territory. . . .

If no efficient international agreement is achieved, the race for nuclear armaments will be on in earnest not later than the morning after our first demonstration of the existence of nuclear weapons. After this, it might take other nations three or four years to overcome our present head start, and eight or ten years to draw even with us if we continue to do intensive work in this field. This might be all the time we would have to bring about the relocation of our population and industry. Obviously, no time should be lost in inaugurating a study of this problem by experts.

Prospects for International Agreement

The consequences of nuclear warfare, and the type of measures which would have to be taken to protect a country from total destruction by nuclear bombing, must be as abhorrent to other nations as to the United States. England, France and the smaller nations of the European continent, with their congeries of people and industries would be in a particularly desperate situation in the face of such a threat. Russia and China are the only great nations at present which could survive a nuclear attack. However, even though these countries may value human life less than the peoples of Western Europe and America, and even though Russia, in particular, has an immense space over which its vital industries could be dispersed and a government which can order this dispersion the day it is convinced that such a measure is necessary—there is no doubt that Russia, too, will shudder at the possibility of a sudden disintegration of Moscow and Leningrad, almost miraculously preserved in the present war, and of its new industrial cities in the Urals and Siberia. Therefore, only lack of mutual trust, and not lack of desire for agreement, can stand in the path of an efficient agreement for the prevention of nuclear warfare. The achievement of such an agreement will thus essentially depend on the integrity of intentions and readiness to sacrifice the necessary fraction of one's own sovereignty, by all the parties to the agreement.

Surprise Attack

One possible way to introduce nuclear weapons to the world—which may particularly appeal to those who consider nuclear bombs primarily as a secret weapon developed to help win the present war—is to use them without warning on appropriately selected objects in Japan.

Although important tactical results undoubtedly can be achieved by a sudden introduction of nuclear weapons, we nevertheless think that the question of the use of the very first available atomic bombs in the Japanese war should be weighed very carefully, not only by military authorities, but by the highest political leadership of this country.

Russia, and even allied countries which bear less mistrust of our ways and intentions, as well as neutral countries may be deeply shocked by this step. It may be very difficult to persuade the world that a nation which was capable of secretly preparing and suddenly releasing a new weapon, as indiscriminate as the rocket bomb and a thousand times more destructive, is to be trusted in its proclaimed desire of having such weapons abolished by international agreement. We have large accumulations of poison gas, but do not use them, and recent polls have shown that public opinion in this country would disapprove of such a use even if it would accelerate the winning of the Far Eastern war. It is true that some irrational element in mass psychology makes gas poisoning more revolting than blasting by explosives, even though gas warfare is in no way more "in-human" than the war of bombs and bullets. Nevertheless, it is not at all certain that American public opinion, if it could be enlightened as to the effect of atomic explosives, would approve of our own country being the first to introduce such an indiscriminate method of wholesale destruction of civilian life.

Thus, from the "optimistic" point of view—looking forward to an international agreement on the prevention of nuclear warfare—the military advantages and the saving of American lives achieved by the sudden use of atomic bombs against Japan may be outweighed by the ensuing loss of confidence and by a wave of horror and repulsion sweeping over the rest of the world and perhaps even dividing public opinion at home.

Demonstration for the United Nations

From this point of view, a demonstration of the new weapon might best be made, before the eyes of representatives of all the United Nations, on the desert or a barren island. The best possible atmosphere for the achievement of an international agreement could be achieved if America could say to the world, "You see what sort of a weapon we had but did not use. We are ready to renounce its use in the future if other nations join us in this renunciation and agree to the establishment of an efficient control."

After such a demonstration the weapon might perhaps be used against Japan if the sanction of the United Nations (and if public opinion at home) were obtained, perhaps after a preliminary ultimatum to Japan to surrender or at least to evacuate certain regions as an alternative to their total destruction. This may sound fantastic, but in nuclear weapons we have something entirely new in order of magnitude of destructive power, and if we want to capitalize fully on the advantage their possession gives us, we must use new and imaginative methods.

It must be stressed that if one takes the pessimistic point of view and discounts the possibility of an effective international control over nuclear weapons at the present time, then the advisability of an early use of nuclear bombs against Japan becomes even more doubtful—quite independently of any humanitarian considerations. If an international agreement is not concluded immediately after the first demonstration, this will mean a flying start towards an unlimited armaments race. If this race is inevitable, we have every reason to delay its beginning as long as possible in order to increase our head start still further. . . .

International Control

We now consider the question of how an effective international control of nuclear armaments can be achieved. This is a difficult problem, but we think it soluble. It requires study by statesmen and international lawyers, and we can offer only some preliminary suggestions for such a study.

Given mutual trust and willingness on all sides to give up a certain part of their sovereign rights, by admitting international control of certain phases of national economy, the control could be exercised (alternatively or simultaneously) on two different levels.

The first and perhaps the simplest way is to ration the raw materials—primarily, the uranium ores. Production of nuclear explosives begins with the processing of large quantities of uranium in large isotope separation plants or huge production piles. The amounts of ore taken out of the ground at different locations could be controlled by resident agents of the international Control Board, and each nation could be allotted only an amount which would make large-scale separation of fissionable isotopes impossible.

Such a limitation would have the drawback of making impossible also the development of nuclear power for peacetime purposes. However, it need not prevent the production of radioactive elements on a scale sufficient to revolutionize the industrial, scientific and technical use of these materials, and would thus not eliminate the main benefits which nucleonics promises to bring to mankind.

An agreement on a higher level, involving more mutual trust and understanding, would be to allow unlimited production, but keep exact bookkeeping on the fate of each pound of uranium mined. If in this way, check is kept on the conversion of uranium and thorium ore into pure fissionable materials, the question arises as to how to prevent accumulation of large quantities of such materials in the hands of one or several nations. Accumulations of this kind could be rapidly converted into atomic bombs if a nation should break away from international control. It has been suggested that a compulsory denaturation of pure fissionable isotopes may be agreed upon—by diluting them, after production, with suitable isotopes to make them useless for military purposes, while retaining their usefulness for power engines.

One thing is clear: any international agreement on prevention of nuclear armaments must be backed by actual and efficient controls. No paper agreement can be sufficient since neither this or any other nation can stake its whole existence on trust in other nations' signatures. Every attempt to impede the international control agencies would have to be considered equivalent to denunciation of the agreement.

It hardly needs stressing that we as scientists believe that any systems of control envisaged should leave as much freedom for the peacetime development of nucleonics as is consistent with the safety of the world.

Future Control

The development of nuclear power not only constitutes an important addition to the technological and military power of the United States, but also creates grave political and economic problems for the future of this country.

Nuclear bombs cannot possibly remain a "secret weapon" at the exclusive disposal of this country for more than a few years. The scientific facts on which construction is based are well known to scientists of other countries. Unless an effective international control of nuclear explosives is instituted, a race for nuclear armaments is certain to ensue following the first revelation of our possession of nuclear weapons to the world. Within ten years other countries may have nuclear bombs, each of which, weighing less than a ton, could destroy an urban area of more than ten square miles. In the war to which such an armaments race is likely to lead, the United States, with its agglomeration of population and industry in comparatively few metropolitan districts, will be at a disadvantage compared to nations whose populations and industry are scattered over large areas.

We believe that these considerations make the use of nuclear bombs for an early unannounced attack against Japan inadvisable. If the United States were to be the first to release this new means of indiscriminate destruction upon mankind, she would sacrifice public support throughout the world, precipitate the race for armaments and prejudice the possibility of reaching an international agreement on the future control of such weapons.

Much more favorable conditions for the eventual achievement of such an agreement could be created if nuclear bombs were first revealed to the world by a demonstration in an appropriately selected uninhabited area.

In case chances for the establishment of an effective international control of nuclear weapons should have to be considered slight at the present time, then not only the use of these weapons against Japan, but even their early demonstration, may be contrary to the interests of this country. A postponement of such a demonstration will have in this case the advantage of delaying the beginning of the nuclear armaments race as long as possible.

If the government should decide in favor of an early demonstration of nuclear weapons, it will then have the possibility of taking into account the public opinion of this country and of the other nations before deciding whether these weapons should be used against Japan. In this way, other nations may assume a share of responsibility for such a fateful decision.

Composed and signed by

J. FRANCK
D. HUGHES
L. SZILARD
T. HOGNESS
E. RABINOWITCH
G. SEABORG
C.J. NICKSON

The Decision to Use the Atomic Bomb

Henry L. Stimson

Henry L. Stimson was Secretary of War for Presidents Franklin D. Roosevelt and Harry S. Truman. He was considered one of the wisest and most knowledgeable men in government. He was also aware of the Manhattan Project from its inception. In the following excerpt, which originally appeared in the February 1947 issue of *Harper's Magazine,* Stimson explains the policies that led to the use of the atomic bomb against Japan in 1945.

From the beginning, Stimson and President Roosevelt decided to pursue an all-out program to be the first nation to develop the atomic bomb and use it to shorten the war. Roosevelt, however, died before the project came to fruition. President Truman took office in 1945 when the bomb was nearing completion. By July of that year, Germany had been defeated and the military was preparing its invasion plans for the Japanese home islands. This campaign was expected to be more bitter and costly than the fight for Germany. American losses might approach 1 million lives. Faced with these kinds of losses, Stimson acknowledged "the position of the atomic bomb in our planning became quite clear." Still, the United States was not eager to use such a devastating weapon and pursued diplomatic channels to show the Japanese the fruitlessness of continued hostilities.

Japan, however, rejected the United States' ultimatum for surrender, and Truman consented to use the new weapon. Stimson attests that his and the administration's support for the bomb's use was to bring victory to the United States with

Excerpted from "The Decision to Use the Atomic Bomb," by Henry L. Stimson, *Harper's Magazine*, February 1947. Copyright © 1947 by Henry L. Stimson. Reprinted by permission of the publisher.

the least possible loss of life. He says, "no man, in our position . . . holding in his hands a weapon . . . for accomplishing this purpose and saving those lives, could have failed to use it and afterwards looked his countrymen in the face."

The policy adopted and steadily pursued by President Roosevelt and his advisers was a simple one. It was to spare no effort in securing the earliest possible successful development of an atomic weapon. The reasons for this policy were equally simple. The original experimental achievement of atomic fission had occurred in Germany in 1938, and it was known that the Germans had continued their experiments. In 1941 and 1942 they were believed to be ahead of us, and it was vital that they should not be the first to bring atomic weapons into the field of battle. Furthermore, if we should be the first to develop the weapon, we should have a great new instrument for shortening the war and minimizing destruction. At no time, from 1941 to 1945, did I ever hear it suggested by the President, or by any other responsible member of the government, that atomic energy should not be used in the war. All of us of course understood the terrible responsibility involved in our attempt to unlock the doors to such a devastating weapon; President Roosevelt particularly spoke to me many times of his own awareness of the catastrophic potentialities of our work. But we were at war, and the work must be done. I therefore emphasize that it was our common objective, throughout the war, to be the first to produce an atomic weapon and use it. The possible atomic weapon was considered to be a new and tremendously powerful explosive, as legitimate as any other of the deadly explosive weapons of modern war. The entire purpose was the production of a military weapon; on no other ground could the wartime expenditure of so much time and money have been justified. The exact circumstances in which that weapon might be used were unknown to any of us until the middle of 1945, and when that time came, as we shall presently see, the military use of atomic energy was connected with larger questions of national policy. . . .

"As time went on it became clear that the weapon would not be available in time for use in the European theater, and the war against Germany was successfully ended by the use of what are now called conventional means. But in the spring of 1945 it became evident that the climax of our prolonged atomic effort was at hand. By the nature of atomic chain reactions, it was impossible to state with certainty that we had succeeded until a bomb had actually exploded in a full-scale experiment; nevertheless it was considered exceedingly probable that we should by midsummer have successfully detonated the first atomic bomb. This was to be done at the Alamogordo Reservation in New Mexico. It was thus time for detailed consideration of our future plans. What had begun as a well-founded hope was now developing into a reality. . . .

The Achievement of Surrender

The principal political, social, and military objective of the United States in the summer of 1945 was the prompt and complete surrender of Japan. Only the complete destruction of her military power could open the way to lasting peace.

Japan, in July, 1945, had been seriously weakened by our increasingly violent attacks. It was known to us that she had gone so far as to make tentative proposals to the Soviet Government, hoping to use the Russians as mediators in a negotiated peace. These vague proposals contemplated the retention by Japan of important conquered areas and were therefore not considered seriously. There was as yet no indication of any weakening in the Japanese determination to fight rather than accept unconditional surrender. If she should persist in her fight to the end, she had still a great military force.

In the middle of July, 1945, the intelligence section of the War Department General Staff estimated Japanese military strength as follows: in the home islands, slightly under 2,000,000; in Korea, Manchuria, China proper, and Formosa, slightly over 2,000,000; in French Indo-China, Thailand, and Burma, over 200,000; in the East Indies area, including the Philippines, over 500,000; in the by-passed Pacific islands, over 100,000. The total strength of the Japanese Army was estimated at about 5,000,000 men. These estimates later proved to be in very close agreement with official Japanese figures.

The Japanese Army was in much better condition than the Japanese Navy and Air Force. The Navy had practically ceased to exist except as a harrying force against an invasion fleet. The Air Force had been reduced mainly to reliance upon Kamikaze, or suicide, attacks. These latter, however, had already inflicted serious damage on our seagoing forces, and their possible effectiveness in a last ditch fight was a matter of real concern to our naval leaders.

As we understood it in July, there was a very strong possibility that the Japanese Government might determine upon resistance to the end, in all the areas of the Far East under its control. In such an event the Allies would be faced with the enormous task of destroying an armed force of five million men and five thousand suicide aircraft, belonging to a race which had already amply demonstrated its ability to fight literally to the death.

The strategic plans of our armed forces for the defeat of Japan, as they stood in July, had been prepared without reliance upon the atomic bomb, which had not yet been tested in New Mexico. We were planning an intensified sea and air blockade, and greatly intensified strategic air bombing, through the summer and early fall, to be followed on November 1 by an invasion of the southern island of Kyushu. This would be followed in turn by an invasion of the main island of Honshu in the spring of 1946. The total U.S. military and naval force involved in this grand design was of the order of 5,000,000 men; if all those indirectly concerned are included, it was larger still. . . .

A Million American Lives

We estimated that if we should be forced to carry this plan to its conclusion, the major fighting would not end until the latter part of 1946, at the earliest. I was informed that such operations might be expected to cost over a million casualties, to American forces alone. Additional large losses might be expected among our allies and, of course, if our campaign were successful and if we could judge by previous experience, enemy casualties would be much larger than our own.

The Atom Bomb and Peace

Admiral William D. Leahy, chief of staff to Presidents Roosevelt and Truman, in his memoir, I Was There, *declares that dropping the atomic bombs on Japan was not necessary. He says that in "being the first to use it, we had adopted an ethical standard common to the barbarians of the Dark Ages." Nevertheless, he concludes that until atomic weapons are governed by international laws, "the United States must have more and better bombs than any potential enemy."*

In the spring of 1945 President Truman directed Mr. Byrnes to make a special study of the status and prospects of the new atomic explosive on which two billion dollars already had been spent. Byrnes came to my home on the evening of June 4 to discuss his findings. He was more favorably impressed than I had been up to that time with the prospects of success in the final development and use of this new weapon.

Once it had been tested, President Truman faced the decision as to whether to use it. He did not like the idea, but was persuaded that it would shorten the war against Japan and save American lives. It is my opinion that the use of this barbarous weapon at Hiroshima and Nagasaki was of no material assistance in our war against Japan. The Japanese were already defeated and ready to surrender because of the effective sea blockade and the successful bombing with conventional weapons.

It was my reaction that the scientists and others wanted to make this test because of the vast sums that had been spent on the project. Truman knew that, and so did the other people involved. However, the Chief Executive made a de-

It was already clear in July that even before the invasion we should be able to inflict enormously severe damage on the Japanese homeland by the combined application of 'conventional' sea and air power. The critical question was whether this kind of action would induce surrender. It therefore became necessary to consider very carefully the prob-

cision to use the bomb on two cities in Japan. We had only produced two bombs at that time. We did not know which cities would be the targets, but the President specified that the bombs should be used against military facilities.

I realized that my original error in discounting the effectiveness of the atomic bomb was based on long experience with explosives in the Navy. I had specialized in gunnery and at one time headed the Navy Department's Bureau of Ordnance. "Bomb" is the wrong word to use for this new weapon. It is not a bomb. It is not an explosive. It is a poisonous thing that kills people by its deadly radioactive reaction, more than by the explosive force it develops.

The lethal possibilities of atomic warfare in the future are frightening. My own feeling was that in being the first to use it, we had adopted an ethical standard common to the barbarians of the Dark Ages. I was not taught to make war in that fashion, and wars cannot be won by destroying women and children. We were the first to have this weapon in our possession, and the first to use it. There is a practical certainty that potential enemies will have it in the future and that atomic bombs will sometime be used against us. . . .

However, I am forced to a reluctant conclusion that for the security of my own country which has been the guiding principle in my approach to all problems faced during my career, there is but one course open to us:

Until the United Nations, or some world organization, can guarantee—and have the power to enforce that guarantee—that the world will be spared the terrors of atomic warfare, the United States must have more and better atom bombs than any potential enemy.

William D. Leahy, *I Was There*. New York: Arno Press, 1979.

able state of mind of the enemy, and to assess with accuracy the line of conduct which might end his will to resist.

With these considerations in mind, I wrote a memorandum for the President [Harry S. Truman], on July 2, which I believe fairly represents the thinking of the American Government as it finally took shape in action. This memorandum was prepared after discussion and general agreement with Joseph C. Grew, Acting Secretary of State, and Secretary of the Navy Forrestal, and when I discussed it with the President, he expressed his general approval.

Memorandum for the President

July 2, 1945

PROPOSED PROGRAM FOR JAPAN

1. The plans of operation up to and including the first landing have been authorized and the preparations for the operation are now actually going on. This situation was accepted by all members of your conference on Monday, June 18.

2. There is reason to believe that the operation for the occupation of Japan following the landing may be a very long, costly, and arduous struggle on our part. The terrain, much of which I have visited several times, has left the impression on my memory of being one which would be susceptible to a last ditch defense such as has been made on Iwo Jima and Okinawa and which of course is very much larger than either of those two areas. According to my recollection it will be much more unfavorable with regard to tank maneuvering than either the Philippines or Germany.

3. If we once land on one of the main islands and begin a forceful occupation of Japan, we shall probably have cast the die of last ditch resistance. The Japanese are highly patriotic and certainly susceptible to calls for fanatical resistance to repel an invasion. Once started in actual invasion, we shall in my opinion have to go through with an even more bitter finish fight than in Germany. We shall incur the losses incident to such a war and we shall have to leave the Japanese islands even more thoroughly destroyed than was the case with Germany. This would be due both to the difference in the Japanese and German personal character and the differences in the size and character of the terrain through which the operations will take place.

4. A question then comes: Is there any alternative to such a

forceful occupation of Japan which will secure for us the equivalent of an unconditional surrender of her forces and a permanent destruction of her power again to strike an aggressive blow at the 'peace of the Pacific'? I am inclined to think that there is enough such chance to make it well worth while our giving them a warning of what is to come and definite opportunity to capitulate. As above suggested, it should be tried before the actual forceful occupation of the homeland islands is begun and furthermore the warning should be given in ample time to permit a national reaction to set in. . . .

5. It is therefore my conclusion that a carefully timed warning be given to Japan by the chief representatives of the United States, Great Britain, China, and, if then a belligerent, Russia, by calling upon Japan to surrender and permit the occupation of her country in order to ensure its complete demilitarization for the sake of the future peace.

This warning should contain the following elements:

The varied and overwhelming character of the force we are about to bring to bear on the islands.

The inevitability and completeness of the destruction which the full application of this force will entail.

The determination of the Allies to destroy permanently all authority and influence of those who have deceived and misled the country into embarking on world conquest.

The determination of the Allies to limit Japanese sovereignty to her main islands and to render them powerless to mount and support another war.

The disavowal of any attempt to extirpate the Japanese as a race or to destroy them as a nation.

A statement of our readiness, once her economy is purged of its militaristic influence, to permit the Japanese to maintain such industries, particularly of a light consumer character, as offer no threat of aggression against their neighbors, but which can produce a sustaining economy, and provide a reasonable standard of living. The statement should indicate our willingness, for this purpose, to give Japan trade access to external raw materials, but not longer any control over the sources of supply outside her main islands. It should also indicate our willingness, in accordance with our now established foreign trade policy, in due course to enter into mutually advantageous trade relations with her.

The withdrawal from their country as soon as the above objectives of the Allies are accomplished, and as soon as there has been established a peacefully inclined government, of a character representative of the masses of the Japanese people. I personally think that if in saying this we should add that we do not exclude a constitutional monarchy under her present dynasty, it would substantially add to the chances of acceptance.

6. Success of course will depend on the potency of the warning which we give her. She has an extremely sensitive national pride, and, as we are now seeing every day, when actually locked with the enemy will fight to the very death. For that reason the warning must be tendered before the actual invasion has occurred and while the impending destruction, though clear beyond peradventure, has not yet reduced her to fanatical despair. If Russia is a part of the threat, the Russian attack, if actual, must not have progressed too far. Our own bombing should be confined to military objectives as far as possible.

HENRY L. STIMSON
Secretary of War.

The Bomb and the Potsdam Ultimatum

It is important to emphasize the double character of the suggested warning. It was designed to promise destruction if Japan resisted, and hope, if she surrendered.

It will be noted that the atomic bomb is not mentioned in this memorandum. On grounds of secrecy the bomb was never mentioned except when absolutely necessary, and furthermore, it had not yet been tested. It was of course well forward in our minds, as the memorandum was written and discussed, that the bomb would be the best possible sanction if our warning were rejected.

The adoption of the policy outlined in the memorandum of July 2 was a decision of high politics; once it was accepted by the President, the position of the atomic bomb in our planning became quite clear. I find that I stated in my diary, as early as June 19, that 'the last chance warning . . . must be given before an actual landing of the ground forces in Japan, and fortunately the plans provide for enough time to bring in the sanctions to our warning in the shape of heavy ordinary bombing attack and an attack of S-1.' S-1 was a code name for the atomic bomb.

There was much discussion in Washington about the timing of the warning to Japan. The controlling factor in the end was the date already set for the Potsdam meeting of the Big Three [Truman, Churchill, and Stalin]. It was President Truman's decision that such a warning should be solemnly issued by the U.S. and the U.K. from this meeting, with the concurrence of the head of the Chinese Government, so that it would be plain that *all* of Japan's principal enemies were in entire unity. This was done, in the Potsdam ultimatum of July 26, which very closely followed the above memorandum of July 2, with the exception that it made no mention of the Japanese Emperor.

On July 28 the Premier of Japan, Suzuki, rejected the Potsdam ultimatum by announcing that it was 'unworthy of public notice.' In the face of this rejection we could only proceed to demonstrate that the ultimatum had meant exactly what it said when it stated that if the Japanese continued the war, 'the full application of our military power, backed by our resolve, will mean the inevitable and complete destruction of the Japanese armed forces and just as inevitably the utter devastation of the Japanese homeland.'

For such a purpose the atomic bomb was an eminently suitable weapon. The New Mexico test occurred while we were at Potsdam, on July 16. It was immediately clear that the power of the bomb measured up to our highest estimates. We had developed a weapon of such a revolutionary character that its use against the enemy might well be expected to produce exactly the kind of shock on the Japanese ruling oligarchy which we desired, strengthening the position of those who wished peace, and weakening that of the military party. . . .

Surrender

Hiroshima was bombed on August 6, and Nagasaki on August 9. These two cities were active working parts of the Japanese war effort. One was an army center; the other was naval and industrial. Hiroshima was the headquarters of the Japanese Army defending southern Japan and was a major military storage and assembly point. Nagasaki was a major seaport and it contained several large industrial plants of great wartime importance. We believed that our attacks had struck cities which must certainly be important to the Japanese military leaders, both Army and Navy, and we waited for a result. We waited one day.

Many accounts have been written about the Japanese surrender. After a prolonged Japanese Cabinet session in which the deadlock was broken by the Emperor himself, the offer to surrender was made on August 10. It was based on the Potsdam terms, with a reservation concerning the sovereignty of the Emperor.

Choosing a Target

the Target Committee

The Target Committee was formed under the command of Brigadier General Leslie Groves, the head of the Manhattan Project. Groves's deputy, Brigadier General Thomas F. Farrell, chaired the committee. The members consisted of two other Air Force commanders and five scientists. The Target Committee, the Interim Committee, and a third committee consisting of Truman's advisers were all formed to make recommendations to the president on how to best use the bomb.

At the end of its two-day meeting on May 10 and 11, 1945, the Target Committee had dealt with a number of important topics surrounding utilizing atomic weapons against Japan. One item was the most effective height at which to detonate such bombs. If a nuclear warhead was exploded too high off the ground, much of its power would be lost in the atmosphere. On the other hand, if the bomb went off too close to the ground, its power would be limited by blowing a crater in the earth. Regarding Fat Man and Little Boy, the two different atomic bombs being prepared for use against Japan, the committee recommended the fuses be set to detonate roughly 1,000 feet from the ground.

The committee also considered possible targets for the mission. These targets were large cities with concentrations of military and industrial resources that were helpful to the Japanese war effort. Kyoto, Hiroshima, Yokohama, and Kokura Arsenal were all offered as worthwhile targets. While Hiroshima was ultimately chosen as the prime target, Nagasaki, the city selected for the second demonstration of nuclear destruction, was not mentioned in this report.

Besides providing suggestions on the use of atomic

Excerpted from *Minutes of the Second Meeting of the Target Committee, May 10–11, 1945* (Washington, DC: U.S. National Archives, 1945).

weapons, the Target Committee also discussed such topics as achieving the greatest psychological effect against the enemy and the safe distance the mission aircraft must maintain from the nuclear blast and radioactive cloud. The completed minutes of the Target Committee meeting were typed up and submitted to Brigadier General Groves on May 12. These conclusions were then taken to a meeting with President Harry Truman where final decisions to use the weapons were made.

M emorandum For: Major General L.R. Groves
Subject: Summary of Target Committee Meetings on 10 and 11 May 1945

The second meeting of the Target Committee convened at 9:00 AM 10 May in Dr. Oppenheimer's office at Site Y with the following present:

General Farrell Dr. C. Lauritsen Colonel Seeman Dr. Ramsey Captain Parsons Dr. Dennison Major Derry Dr. von Neumann Dr. Stearns Dr. Wilson Dr. Tolman Dr. Penney Dr. Oppenheimer

Dr. Bethe and Dr. Brode were brought into the meeting for discussion of Item A of the agenda. During the course of the meeting panels were formed from the committee members and others to meet in the afternoon and develop conclusions to items discussed in the agenda. The concluding meeting was held at 10:00 AM 11 May in Dr. Oppenheimer's office with the following present:

Colonel Seemand
Dr. Stearns
Captain Parsons
Dr. von Neumann
Major Derry
Dr. Dennison
Dr. Tolman
Dr. Penney
Dr. Oppenheimer
Dr. Ramsey
Dr. Wilson

The agenda for the meetings presented by Dr. Oppenheimer consisted of the following: . . .

Height of Detonation

A. The criteria for determining height selection were discussed. It was agreed that conservative figures should be used in determining the height since it is not possible to predict accurately the magnitude of the explosion and since the bomb can be detonated as much as 40% below the optimum with a reduction of 25% in area of damage whereas a detonation 14% above the optimum will cause the same loss in area. . . .

B. In the case of the Fat Man delay circuits are introduced into the unit for purposes which make the detonation of the bomb 400 feet below the height at which the fuse is set. For this reason as far as the Fat Man is concerned the fuse settings should be 980 feet, 1,400 feet, or 1,950 feet.

C. In view of the above it was agreed by all present that fuses should be available at four (4) different height settings. These heights are 1,000 feet, 1,400 feet, 2,000 feet and 2,400 feet. With present information the 1,400 feet fuse would be most likely to be used for both the Fat Man and the Little Boy. (Later data presented by Dr. Brode modify the above conclusions on fusing and detonating heights; the differential height for the Little Boy is 210 feet and for the Fat Man 500 feet. For this reason some of the above figures must be revised).

Report on Weather and Operations

A. Dr. Dennison reported on the above subject. His report essentially covered the materials in his Top Secret memo of 9 May—Subject: "Preliminary report on Operational Procedures". For this reason his report will not be repeated here but is attached as an appendix. It was agreed by those present that the mission if at all possible should be a visual bombing mission. For this we should be prepared to wait until there is a good weather forecast in one or more of three alternative targets. There is only a 2% chance in this case that we will have to wait over two weeks. When the mission does take place there should be weather spotter aircraft over each of three alternative targets in order that an alternative target may be selected in the last hour of the flight if the weather is unpromising over the highest priority target.

B. In case the aircraft reaches the target and finds, despite these precautions that visual bombing is impossible, it should return to its base provided that it is in good operating condition. Only if the aircraft is in sufficiently bad shape that it is unlikely that it can return to base and make a safe landing or if it is essential that the drop be made that day should the drop be made with radar equipment. For this purpose it may be desirable to have an Eagle radar equipped plane accompany the mission in order that formation bombing with the Eagle plane in the lead can be made to obtain the increased accuracy from Eagle. A final decision as to the desirability of this emergency procedure can only be made after further combat experience is obtained with Eagle aircraft. In any case every effort should be made to have the mission such that blind bombing will be unnecessary.

C. It was agreed that Dr. Stearns and Dr. Dennison should keep themselves continuously informed as to radar developments. If at any time new developments are available which show in combat a marked improvement of accuracy the basic plan may be altered.

D. It was agreed that Shoran [a type of radar] was a very promising development for the 21st Bomber Command but that we should make no plans to use Shoran until its success is fully confirmed in normal bombing missions in that area.

E. The plan to use the gadget with visual bombing even though this may require a one day to three weeks delay requires that the gadget be such that for a period of at least three weeks it can be held in readiness in such a state that on twelve hours notice it can be prepared for a combat mission. No difficulty in this regard was foreseen by those present.

Gadget Jettisoning and Landing

A. It was agreed that if the aircraft has to return to its base with the gadget and if it is in good condition when it has reached there, it should make a normal landing with the greatest possible care and with such precautions as stand-by fire equipment being held in readiness on the ground. This operation will inevitably involve some risks to the base and to the other aircraft parked on the field. However, the chance of a crash when the aircraft is in good condition and the chances of a crash initiating a high order explosion are both sufficiently small that it was the view of those present that the landing operation with the unit under these circumstances was a justifiable risk. Frequent landings with inert and H.E. filled units have been made in the past. Training in landing with the unit should be given to all crews who carry an active unit.

B. In case the aircraft returns to its base and then finds that it cannot make a normal landing it may be necessary to jettison the bomb. In the case of the Fat Man this can probably best be accomplished by dropping the bomb into shallow water from a low altitude. Tests on this will be carried out with both inert and live units. In the case of the Little Boy the situation is considerably more complicated since water leaking into the Little Boy will set off a nuclear reaction, and since the American held territory in the vicinity of the base is so densely filled that no suitable jettisoning ground for the Little Boy has been found which is sufficiently devoid of moisture, which is sufficiently soft that the projectile is sure not to seat from the impact, and which is sufficiently remote from extremely important American installations whose damage by a nuclear explosion would seriously affect the American war effort. The best emergency procedure that has so far been proposed is considered to be the removal of the gunpowder from the gun and the execution of a crash landing. In this case there is no danger of fire setting off the gun and the accelerations should be sufficiently small to prevent seating of the projectile by the impact. Tests on the feasibility of unloading the gun powder in flight will be conducted.

C. It was agreed that prior to actual delivery some form of instructions should be prepared as a guide to the senior man on the aircraft as to procedures to be followed in cases of different types of disasters.

Status of Targets

A. Dr. Stearns described the work he had done on target selection. He has surveyed possible targets possessing the following qualification: (1) they be important targets in a large urban area of more than three miles in diameter, (2) they be capable of being damaged effectively by a blast, and (3) they are unlikely to be attacked by next August. Dr. Stearns had a list of five targets which the Air Force would be willing to reserve for our use unless unforeseen circumstances arise. These targets are:

(1) **Kyoto**—This target is an urban industrial area with a population of 1,000,000. It is the former capital of Japan and many people and industries are now being moved there as other areas are being destroyed. From the psychological point of view there is the advantage that Kyoto is an intellectual center for Japan and the people there are more apt to appreciate the significance of such a weapon as the gadget. (Classified as an AA Target)

(2) **Hiroshima**—This is an important army depot and port of embarkation in the middle of an urban industrial area. It is a good radar target and it is such a size that a large part of the city could be extensively damaged. There are adjacent hills which are likely to produce a focussing effect which would considerably increase the blast damage. Due to rivers it is not a good incendiary target. (Classified as an AA Target)

(3) **Yokohama**—This target is an important urban industrial area which has so far been untouched. Industrial activities include aircraft manufacture, machine tools, docks, electrical equipment and oil refineries. As the damage to Tokyo has increased additional industries have moved to Yokohama. It has the disadvantage of the most important target areas being separated by a large body of water and of being in the heaviest anti-aircraft concentration in Japan. For us it has the advantage as an alternate target for use in case

of bad weather of being rather far removed from the other targets considered. (Classified as an A Target)

(4) **Kokura Arsenal**—This is one of the largest arsenals in Japan and is surrounded by urban industrial structures. The arsenal is important for light ordnance, anti-aircraft and beach head defense materials. The dimensions of the arsenal are 4100' × 2000'. The dimensions are such that if the bomb were properly placed full advantage could be taken of the higher pressures immediately underneath the bomb for destroying the more solid structures and at the same time considerable blast damage could be done to more feeble structures further away. (Classified as an A Target)

(5) **Niigata**—This is a port of embarkation on the N.W. coast of Honshu. Its importance is increasing as other ports are damaged. Machine tool industries are located there and it is a potential center for industrial dispersion. It has oil refineries and storage. (Classified as a B Target)

(6) The possibility of bombing the Emperor's palace was discussed. It was agreed that we should not recommend it but that any action for this bombing should come from authorities on military policy. It was agreed that we should obtain information from which we could determine the effectiveness of our weapon against this target.

B. It was the recommendation of those present at the meeting that the first four choices of targets for our weapon should be the following:

    a. Kyoto
    b. Hiroshima
    c. Yokohama
    d. Kokura Arsenal

C. Dr. Stearns agreed to do the following: (1) brief Colonel Fisher thoroughly on these matters, (2) request reservations for these targets, (3) find out more about the target area including exact locations of the strategic industries there, (4) obtain further photo information on the targets, and (5) to determine the nature of the construction, the area, heights, contents and roof coverage of buildings. He also agreed to keep in touch with the target data as it develops and to keep the committee advised of other possible target areas. He will also check on locations of small military targets and obtain further details on the Emperor's palace.

Psychological Factors in Target Selection

A. It was agreed that psychological factors in the target selection were of great importance. Two aspects of this are (1) obtaining the greatest psychological effect against Japan and (2) making the initial use sufficiently spectacular for the importance of the weapon to be internationally recognized when publicity on it is released.

B. In this respect Kyoto has the advantage of the people being more highly intelligent and hence better able to appreciate the significance of the weapon. Hiroshima has the advantage of being such a size and with possible focussing from nearby mountains that a large fraction of the city may be destroyed. The Emperor's palace in Tokyo has a greater fame than any other target but is of least strategic value.

Use Against "Military" Objectives

A. It was agreed that for the initial use of the weapon any small and strictly military objective should be located in a much larger area subject to blast damage in order to avoid undue risks of the weapon being lost due to bad placing of the bomb.

Radiological Effect

A. Dr. Oppenheimer presented a memo he had prepared on the radiological effects of the gadget. This memo will not be repeated in this summary but it is being sent to General Groves as a separate exhibit. The basic recommendations of this memo are (1) for radiological reasons no aircraft should be closer than 2-1/2 miles to the point of detonation (for blast reasons the distance should be greater) and (2) aircraft must avoid the cloud of radio-active materials. If other aircraft are to conduct missions shortly after the detonation a monitoring plane should determine the areas to be avoided.

Coordinated Air Operations

A. The feasibility of following the raid by an incendiary mission [an air raid using incendiary bombs] was discussed. This has the great advantage that the enemies' fire fighting ability will probably be paralyzed by the gadget so that a very serious conflagration should be capable of being started. However, until more is learned about the phenomena associated with a detonation of the gadget, such as the extent to which there will be radio-active clouds, an incendiary mission immediately after the delivery of the gadget should be avoided. A coordinated incendiary raid should be feasible on the following day at which time the fire raid should still be quite effective. By delaying the coordinated raid to the following day, the scheduling of our already contemplated operations will not be made even more difficult, photo reconnaissance of the actual damage directly caused by our device can be obtained without confusion from the subsequent fire raid, and dangers from radio-active clouds can be avoided.

B. Fighter cover should be used for the operation as directed by the 21st Bomber Command.

Rehearsals

A. It was agreed by all that very complete rehearsals of the entire operation are essential to its success. It is possible for thirty (30) pumpkin units [dummy bombs] for this purpose to be shipped from this country in June with perhaps sixty (60) being shipped in July. These rehearsals overseas should take place beginning in July. At least some of the rehearsals should be very complete including the placing of spotter aircraft over the alternative targets, use of fighter cover, etc. Even though it is hoped that radar will not be used some rehearsals of radar operations are required in order that the operations may be carried out successfully if emergency arises for which they are required.

A. Dr. Penney reported some very encouraging information he had just received from England in this respect. His previous information was that no one could guarantee the safety of a large aircraft at blast pressures greater than 1/2 lb. per square inch. However, in some recent experiments in England large aircraft have been flown over detonations of 2,000 lbs. of TNT and pilots have not objected to going as low as 900 feet. On this basis with a 100,000 ton total equivalent energy release or a 64,000 ton equivalent blast energy 23,000 feet would be a safe altitude on the basis of these experiments if allowance is made for the rarefaction of the atmosphere at high altitudes. However, due to the greater duration of the blast in our case, the safe height will probably be somewhat greater.

Coordination with 21st Program

A. This matter was included as part of the other discussion and is included in previous paragraphs of this summary.

It was agreed that the next meeting of the Target Committee should take place at 9:00 AM EWT on 28 May in Room 4E200 of the Pentagon Building in Washington. Dr. Oppenheimer recommended and others agreed that either Captain Parsons and/or Dr. Ramsey should attend this meeting.

In view of the high classification of the minutes of this meeting it was agreed that copies should not be sent to those present but that instead one copy should be kept on file in General Groves' office, one copy in Dr. Oppenheimer's office, and one copy in Captain Parsons' office.

[signature]
[signature]
Major J.A. Derry
Dr. N.F. Ramsey
Distribution:
Copy 1: Maj Gen L.R. Groves
Copy 2: Capt. Parsons
Copies 3 & 4: J.R. Oppenheimer

Dropping the Atom Bomb

Paul W. Tibbets Jr.

Paul W. Tibbets Jr. was the Air Force pilot of the B-29
bomber that dropped the first atom bomb. He named his plane
after his mother, *Enola Gay*, because she said he would never
be harmed while flying. Tibbets's crew consisted of bombardier Tom Ferebee, navigator "Dutch" Van Kirk, copilot
Bob Lewis, tail-gunner Bob Caron, radar operator Joseph Stiborik, radio operator Richard Nelson, explosives expert Mor-
ris Jeppson, and weaponeer Deak Parsons. The *Enola Gay*
was specially modified to carry the bomb called "Little Boy."
This bomb was 10½ feet long, 29 inches in diameter, and
weighed more than 9,000 pounds. "Little Boy" was a gun-
type nuclear weapon, in which a bullet of uranium 235 is
fired at a target ring of uranium 235 at the end of the bomb,
creating a critical mass and the explosion.

At 2:45 A.M. on August 6, 1945, the *Enola Gay* took off
from Tinian, a Pacific island in the volcanic chain of the Marianas, 1,500 miles east of Tokyo, Japan. As they came closer to
Japan, they flew over Iwo Jima, an island that had recently
been taken from the Japanese in a bitter battle by U.S. Marines.
It is at this point that Tibbets begins his narrative in the following selection from his autobiography, *The Tibbets Story*.

At 7:30 A.M. Parsons armed the bomb. By 9:00 A.M. they
were approaching Hiroshima. No Japanese fighters flew up to
intercept them and there was no antiaircraft fire. The bombardier took control of the plane when he sighted the target—a
bridge on the Ota River in central Hiroshima. Nearby was the

Excerpted from *The Tibbets Story*, by Paul W. Tibbets Jr. with Clair C. Stebbins and Harry
Franken (New York: Stein and Day, 1978). Copyright © 1978 by Paul W. Tibbets, Clair
C. Stebbins, and Harry Franken. Reprinted with permission.

Japanese Second Army headquarters. The bomb-bay doors opened and "Little Boy" fell. "Fellows," Tibbets announced to the crew, "you have just dropped the first atomic bomb in history." Tibbets went on to become a Brigadier General in the Air Force and retired from service in 1966.

The sun flamed red above the eastern horizon almost at the moment we completed our Iwo Jima rendezvous. We had viewed the island through the half-light of predawn and now we were winging toward Japan, surrounded by scattered clouds that were edged with reddish gold from the slanting light of the newly risen sun.

Our course changed leftward by 14 degrees until we were at a compass heading of 322–325, or almost northwest. This would bring us to the island of Shikoku, beyond which lay the city of Hiroshima near the southern tip of Japan's main island of Honshu. Whether this industrial city would become our target depended on the word we would soon receive from our three weather planes, which had taken off from Tinian a little more than an hour ahead of us.

These were *Straight Flush*, piloted by Major Claude Eatherly, which headed for Hiroshima; *Jabbitt III*, commanded by Major John Wilson, en route to the secondary target, Kokura; and *Full House*, Major Ralph Taylor's plane, which had been assigned to check the weather over Nagasaki.

If the first priority target was found to be obscured by clouds, we would turn westward to Kokura or Nagasaki on the coast of Kyushu, a somewhat smaller island to the southwest.

We began to have some misgivings when a thin layer of clouds appeared beneath us. Our orders were for a visual bombing run. Even though radar sighting had proved accurate throughout the war, it had been decided that this bomb should be dropped only if the target was clearly visible. If weather conditions proved unfavorable over all three designated targets we would return with the bomb, but only after it had been disarmed by Deak Parsons. . . .

Armed and Ready

At 7:30, Deak Parsons made some adjustments on the console that controlled the bomb's intricate circuitry. He informed us that the bomb was armed and ready. Bob Lewis wrote on his tablet: "The bomb is now alive. It is a funny feeling knowing it is right in back of you. Knock wood."

Bob expressed the fear that we might encounter weather of such turbulence en route that it would set off the bomb. If so, there wouldn't have been a scrap of aluminum left or a fragment of humanity. The airplane and all of us who were in it would have been atomized. I had no such unpleasant concerns because, even though the mechanics of nuclear fission were a mystery to me, I was aware through briefings at Los Alamos that the system could not be triggered except by the firing of a powerful explosive within the bomb itself.

The next hour was one of suspense as we droned toward the enemy homeland. Without waiting for the weather word, I climbed slowly toward what was to be our bombing altitude of 30,700 feet.

"It's Hiroshima"

We were almost at this level when, at 8:30, the awaited message came in code from Eatherly's *Straight Flush*, high over Hiroshima. As tapped out by Sgt. Pasquale Baldasaro aboard that plane, and taken down on his pad by our radio operator, Dick Nelson, the message consisted of these cryptic letter-figure combinations: "Y-3, Q-3, B-2, C-1."

Bending over Nelson as he wrote, I translated the message to mean that the cloud cover was less than three-tenths at all altitudes. "C-1" was advice, quite unnecessary under the circumstances, to bomb the primary target.

After acknowledging the message, I returned to the controls and strained for the first sight of land ahead. Sweeney and Marquardt, whose planes were accompanying the *Enola Gay* in formation, also received the message and there was no need to break the radio silence that our little group had maintained.

Over the intercom, I gave the word to members of our

crew. "It's Hiroshima," I said.

Within a few minutes, the island of Shikoku came into view. It was 8:30 when we arrived over the shoreline. Our recent tactic of sending flights of one, two, or three planes into the area without dropping bombs was paying dividends. The Japanese had become indifferent toward American aircraft flying at high altitudes on missions they did not understand. They saw no need to waste scarce ammunition, or fuel for interceptor planes, on these apparently harmless visitors.

We flew across Shikoku toward a narrow body of water called the Iyo Sea. Our destination lay just beyond.

Dutch Van Kirk's navigation had been accurate. The airplane was functioning well and, from the green lights on the black box over which Parsons and Jeppson hovered, it was apparent that the bomb circuitry was in order. Parsons tested it frequently.

Below were the scattered clouds that the weather plane had reported—not enough to hinder a visual bomb drop. We were glad that we didn't have to accept an alternate because this was the target for which we had prepared exhaustively for the past week. We had studied maps and aerial photographs of the approach path and the city of Hiroshima. We knew every feature of the terrain over which we would be flying. And now the Japanese landscape was unfolding below us just as the pictures had promised.

We were eight minutes away from the scheduled time of bomb release when the city came into view. The early morning sunlight glistened off the white buildings in the distance. Although I was sure this was our target, there were other cities in the area and I wanted my judgment corroborated. I remembered a pharmacist of my acquaintance who always required an assistant to verify the label on every bottle before mixing a prescription. "Do you all agree that's Hiroshima?" I asked the other crewmen. They promptly concurred.

Initial Point

Now it became our task to find that geographical position on the ground from which the actual bomb run was to begin. This was the Initial Point, or I.P., as it is known to the bombardier. Our I.P., an easily identifiable landmark that stood out in the aerial photos, was 15½ miles east of the point in the heart of the city which was to be our target.

Just south and west of the I.P., which we spotted without difficulty, I made a leftward turn of 60 degrees and came over the point at a heading of 264 degrees, flying almost due west. The reason for this approach, and the reason we had chosen an I.P. to the east of our target, was that the prevailing winds in this area were known to be from the west. It was desirable, from the standpoint of accuracy, to make a bomb run against the wind.

On this important morning, however, the wind was from the south at 10 miles an hour. This was an unpredictable variance, of course. In our planning, we had played the odds and lost.

But Tom Ferebee was an old hand at dropping bombs with the wind, against it, or in a crosswind. From long experience, he knew what a falling bomb would do under almost any condition, and he knew how to crank all the right information into his Norden bomb sight. It made little difference to him that we were delivering a bomb of tremendous size, unlike any that had ever been dropped in warfare. Its shape was even unlike the "pumpkins" [dummy bombs] with which we had practiced over the Utah desert. As I have explained, it had been decided that the first bomb would be as foolproof as possible. Thus the more slender uranium "Little Boy" was chosen over the more complicated plutonium "Fat Man," which was to be used against Nagasaki later the same week.

Although by now we were all concentrating on the bomb run, Dutch Van Kirk found time to note in the plane's log that eight large ships were anchored in a nearby harbor. We were relieved, of course, that no enemy planes had come up to challenge us and that no flak was visible, although frankly, from the experience of our reconaissance flights into the area, we had expected none.

As we zeroed in on the target ahead, I took the microphone and reminded all the crewmen to put on their goggles. They were to keep them poised on their foreheads until the bomb was released, at which time the heavy dark Polaroids were to be slipped over their eyes to protect them from the blinding glare of the bomb blast, which was calculated to have the intensity of 10 suns. In Sweeney's *The Great Artiste* and Marquardt's No. 91, which had dropped back a bit during our approach, the same order was being given.

All that was necessary, upon reaching the I.P., was to fly the predetermined heading, with calculated allowance for the direction (170 degrees) and velocity (8 knots) of the wind. Since we were flying under visual conditions, the problem was simplified. The three-minute run gave Ferebee time to kill the drift and establish a perfectly stable platform for release of the bomb.

Deak Parsons came forward and looked over my shoulder and so did Van Kirk, who was exchanging conversation with Ferebee in the nose of the plane. Navigator and bombardier compared notes and agreed that our ground speed was 285 knots (330 mph) and the drift to the right required an 8-degree correction. Adjustments were made to the bomb sight, which was now engaged to the autopilot for the bomb run. Ferebee, Van Kirk, and I were working as a team, as we had many times before over Europe and North Africa. As we approached the city, we strained our eyes to find the designated aiming point.

From a distance of 10 miles, Ferebee suddenly said, "Okay, I've got the bridge." He pointed dead ahead, where it was just becoming visible. Van Kirk, looking over his shoulders, agreed. "No question about it," he said, scanning an airphoto and comparing it with what he was seeing.

The T-shaped bridge was easy to spot. Even though there were many other bridges in this sprawling city, there was no other bridge that even slightly resembled it.

Van Kirk's job was finished so he went back and sat down, hooking up his safety belt and getting on the interphone.

In this tense moment, Lewis found time to scratch a few

more words in his log: "As we are approaching our primary, Ferebee, Van Kirk, and Stiborik are coming into their own, while the Colonel and I are standing by and giving the boys what they want."

Now it was up to Tom and me. We were only 90 seconds from bomb release when I turned the plane over to him on autopilot.

"It's all yours," I told him, removing my hands from the controls and sliding back a bit in my seat in a not very successful effort to relax. My eyes were fixed on the center of the city, which shimmered in the early morning sunlight.

In the buildings and on the streets there were people, of course, but from 6 miles up they were invisible. To the men who fly the bombers, targets are inanimate, consisting of buildings, bridges, docks, factories, railroad yards. The tragic consequences to humanity are erased from one's thoughts in wartime because war itself is a human tragedy.

Of course, one hopes that civilians will have the good sense to seek protection in bomb shelters. In the case of Hiroshima, I was to learn later that Eatherly's weather plane, over the city three-quarters of an hour before our arrival, had set off air raid sirens but, when nothing happened, ours were ignored. . . .

"Little Boy" Is Dropped

"We're on target," [Tom Ferebee] said, confirming that the sighting and release mechanism were synchronized, so that the drop would take place automatically at a precalculated point in our bomb run.

At 17 seconds after 9:14 A.M., just 60 seconds before the scheduled bomb release, he flicked a toggle switch that activated a high-pitched radio tone. This tone, ominous under the circumstances, sounded in the headphones of the men aboard our plane and the two airplanes that were with us; it was also heard by the men in the three weather planes, which were already more than 200 miles away on their return flight to Tinian.

A moment before, Bob Lewis had made this notation in

his informal log of the flight: "There will be a short intermission while we bomb our target."

Exactly one minute after it began, the radio tone ceased and at the same instant there was the sound of the pneumatic bomb-bay doors opening automatically. Out tumbled "Little Boy," a misnamed package of explosive force infinitely more devastating than any bomb or cluster of bombs ever dropped before.

By my watch, the time was 9:15 plus 17 seconds. In Hiroshima, it was 8:15. We had crossed a time zone in our flight from Tinian.

Much has been made of the fact that we arrived over the target and released our bomb after a 2,000-mile flight just 17 seconds behind the prearranged target time of 9:15. "Uncanny," wrote one correspondent, who mentioned my reputation as "a perfectionist." Actually, we pretended to be upset over the 17-second error, for operational perfection had indeed been the goal of the entire 509th.

Escaping the Blast

With the release of the bomb, the plane was instantly 9,000 pounds lighter. As a result, its nose leaped up sharply and I had to act quickly to execute the most important task of the flight: to put as much distance as possible between our plane and the point at which the bomb would explode.

The 155 degree diving turn to the right, with its 60 degree bank, put a great strain on the airplane and its occupants. Bob Caron, in his tail-gunner's station, had a wild ride that he described as something like being the last man in a game of crack-the-whip.

When we completed the turn, we had lost 1,700 feet and were heading away from our target with engines at full power. Midway through the turn, with its steep bank, it was necessary to back off on the ailerons (other pilots will understand this) to avoid the danger of a roll. I was flying this biggest of all bombers as if it were a fighter plane.

Bob Lewis and I had slipped our dark glasses over our eyes, as I had directed the other crewmen to do, but we promptly discovered that they made it impossible to fly the plane through this difficult getaway maneuver because the instrument panel was blacked out. We pushed the glasses back on our foreheads in a what-the-hell manner, realizing that we would be flying away from the actual flash when it occurred. Ferebee, in the bombardier's position in the nose of the plane, became so fascinated with watching the bomb's free-fall that he forgot all about the glasses. . . .

For me, struggling with the controls, the 43 seconds from bomb release to explosion passed quickly. To some in the plane, it seemed an eternity. Jeppson was quoted as saying that he had counted down the seconds in his mind, apparently too fast, and had the sickening feeling that the bomb was a dud.

Whatever our individual thoughts, it was a period of suspense. I was concentrating so intently on flying the airplane that the flash did not have the impact on my consciousness that one might think, even though it did light up the interior of the plane for a long instant.

There was a startling sensation other than visual, however, that I remember quite vividly to this day. My teeth told me, more emphatically than my eyes, of the Hiroshima explosion.

At the moment of the blast, there was a tingling sensation in my mouth and the very definite taste of lead upon my tongue. This, I was told later by scientists, was the result of electrolysis—an interaction between the fillings in my teeth and the radioactive forces that were loosed by the bomb.

Detonation and Shock Wave

"Little Boy" exploded at the preset altitude of 1,890 feet above the ground, but Bob Caron in the tail was the only one aboard our plane to see the incredible fireball that, in its atom-splitting fury, was a boiling furnace with an inner temperature calculated to be one hundred million degrees Fahrenheit.

Caron, looking directly at the flash through glasses so dense that the sun penetrated but faintly, thought for a moment that he must have been blinded. Ferebee, without glasses but facing in the opposite direction from a relatively exposed position, felt as if a giant flashbulb had gone off a few feet from his face.

I continued my course from the target, awaiting the shock wave, which required almost a minute to reach us. We were racing eastward away from Hiroshima, as was Chuck Sweeney in *The Great Artiste.* Sweeney had made a similar 155 degree turn, but to the left, as soon as he had dropped the instrument packages. Because his plane was charged with the photographic assignment, Marquardt had lagged behind, with movie and still cameras poised to make a record on film of the historic scene.

We must have been 9 miles from the point of the explosion when the shock wave reached us. This was the moment for which we had been bracing ourselves. Would the plane withstand the blow? The scientists were confident that it would, yet they admitted there were some aspects of the nuclear weapon's behavior about which they were not quite certain.

Caron, the only man aboard the plane with an immediate view of the awesome havoc we had created, tried to describe it to us. Suddenly he saw the shock wave approaching at the speed of sound—almost 1,100 feet a second. Condensing moisture from the heated air at the leading edge of the shock wave made it quite visible, just as one sees shimmering air rising from the ground on a hot, humid day.

Before Caron could warn us to brace ourselves, the wave struck the plane with violent force. Our B-29 trembled under the impact and I gripped the controls tightly to keep us in level flight. From my experience of flying through enemy flak over targets in Europe and Africa, I found the effect to be much like that produced by an anti-aircraft shell exploding near the plane.

In fact, that's what Deak Parsons first thought had happened. "It's flak," he shouted, then realized like the rest of us that it was the result we had been told to expect. At a news conference next day, Bob Lewis told reporters that it felt as if some giant had struck the plane with a telephone pole. Soon after the first shock, a second struck us. It was of lesser impact, caused by what the scientists described as "an echo effect."

Mushroom Cloud and the Burning City

Now that I knew we were safe from the effects of the blast, I began circling so that we could view the results. For the record, I announced over the intercom, "Fellows, you have just dropped the first atomic bomb in history."

Caron had been trying to describe what he saw, meanwhile using a hand-held K-20 aerial camera to photograph the scene. He was not a professional photographer and only a few of his pictures proved useful. But many excellent shots were obtained from the photo plane that accompanied us.

Although Caron had told of a mushroom-shaped cloud, and said that it seemed to be "coming toward us," we were not prepared for the awesome sight that met our eyes as we turned for a heading that would take us alongside the burning, devastated city.

The giant purple mushroom, which the tail-gunner had described, had already risen to a height of 45,000 feet, 3 miles above our own altitude, and was still boiling upward like something terribly alive. It was a frightening sight, and even though we were several miles away, it gave the appearance of something that was about to engulf us.

Even more fearsome was the sight on the ground below. At the base of the cloud, fires were springing up everywhere amid a turbulent mass of smoke that had the appearance of bubbling hot tar. If Dante had been with us in the plane, he would have been terrified! The city we had seen so clearly in the sunlight a few minutes before was now an ugly smudge. It had completely disappeared under this awful blanket of smoke and fire.

A feeling of shock and horror swept over all of us.

"My God!" Lewis wrote as the final entry in his log.

He was later quoted as having said. "My God, what have we done?" These words were put in my mouth by the authors of the movie script for *Above and Beyond*.

Whatever exclamations may have passed our lips at this

historic moment, I cannot accurately remember. We were all appalled and what we said was certain to have reflected our emotions and our disbelief. . . .

As we viewed the awesome spectacle below, we were sobered by the knowledge that the world would never be the same. War, the scourge of the human race since time began, now held terrors beyond belief. I reflected to myself that the kind of war in which I was engaged over Europe in 1942 was now outdated.

But as I swung southward on the return flight to our base, the feeling of tenseness gave way to one of relief. Our mission, for which we had practiced diligently for so long, had been successful. All doubts about the mystery weapon had been removed.

"I think this is the end of the war," I said to Bob Lewis as I tamped the tobacco in my pipe bowl and lighted it up once more.

I jotted down a few words on a note pad, tore off the sheet, and handed it to Dick Nelson for radio transmission back to headquarters. In previously agreed-upon phrases, it simply advised that the primary target had been bombed visually with good results and that there had been no fighter opposition or anti-aircraft fire.

Meanwhile Captain Parsons was preparing his own report, containing more detail even though quite brief. Transmitted in code, his message said: "82 V 670. Able, Line 1, Line 2, Line 6, Line 9."

General Farrell, on Tinian, translated it for members of his staff and the scientists who surrounded him: "Clear cut, successful in all respects. Visual effects greater than Trinity. Hiroshima. Conditions normal in airplane following delivery. Proceeding to regular base."

A President's Responsibility

Harry S. Truman

In 1945 Harry S. Truman assumed the presidency after President Roosevelt died while in office. Due to the extreme secrecy surrounding the Manhattan Project, Truman had no previous knowledge of the atomic bomb. He was suddenly confronted with the awesome decision to use "a weapon that would not only revolutionize war but could alter the course of history and civilization." Truman set up a committee of top scientists and advisers "to study with great care the implications the new weapon might have for us."

Truman fully realized that the bomb would inflict unimaginable causalities on the Japanese population, but the invasion of Japan with conventional forces would be far more costly—potentially hundreds of thousands of American and Japanese lives would be lost. Truman's committee recommended the bomb be used against Japan without a specific warning, but the decision to use the bomb could not be made by the military, Congress, or a committee of advisers. It was ultimately up to the president of the United States to make the final decision. At the Potsdam Conference (held outside of Berlin, Germany), where the fate of recently defeated Germany was being decided, Truman did issue a public warning to Japan to cease all hostilities, though he did not reveal that reprisal would come in the form of an atomic weapon. When Japan did not heed the warning, Truman gave the order to use the bomb.

When Truman first received the news of the Hiroshima detonation on August 6, 1945, while on board ship coming

Excerpted from *Memoirs: Volume One: Year of Decisions*, by Harry S. Truman (Garden City, NY: Doubleday & Company Inc., 1955). Copyright © 1955 by Doubleday, a division of Random House. Reprinted with permission.

back from the Potsdam Conference, he said, "This is the greatest thing in history." The explosion was an even greater success than expected. Still the Japanese did not capitulate. A second bomb was dropped over Nagasaki on August 9, and soon after the Japanese Empire surrendered. This account of those fateful days and the president's equally fateful decision comes from the first volume of Truman's *Memoirs*.

The historic message of the first explosion of an atomic bomb was flashed to me in a message from Secretary of War Stimson on the morning of July 16. The most secret and the most daring enterprise of the war had succeeded. We were now in possession of a weapon that would not only revolutionize war but could alter the course of history and civilization. This news reached me at Potsdam the day after I had arrived for the conference of the Big Three.

Preparations were being rushed for the test atomic explosion at Alamogordo, New Mexico, at the time I had to leave for Europe, and on the voyage over I had been anxiously awaiting word on the results. I had been told of many predictions by the scientists, but no one was certain of the outcome of this full-scale atomic explosion. As I read the message from Stimson, I realized that the test not only met the most optimistic expectation of the scientists but that the United States had in its possession an explosive force of unparalleled power.

Stimson flew to Potsdam the next day to see me and brought with him the full details of the test. I received him at once and called in Secretary of State Byrnes, Admiral Leahy, General Marshall, General Arnold, and Admiral King to join us at my office at the Little White House. We reviewed our military strategy in the light of this revolutionary development. We were not ready to make use of this weapon against the Japanese, although we did not know as yet what effect the new weapon might have, physically or psychologically, when used against the enemy. For that reason the military advised that we go ahead with the existing military plans for the invasion of the Japanese home islands.

At Potsdam, as elsewhere, the secret of the atomic bomb was kept closely guarded. We did not extend the very small circle of Americans who knew about it. [British Prime Minister Winston] Churchill naturally knew about the atomic bomb project from its very beginning, because it had involved the pooling of British and American technical skill.

On July 24 I casually mentioned to [Soviet leader Josef] Stalin that we had a new weapon of unusual destructive force. The Russian Premier showed no special interest. All he said was that he was glad to hear it and hoped we would make "good use of it against the Japanese."

Plans for Invasion

A month before the test explosion of the atomic bomb the service Secretaries and the Joint Chiefs of Staff had laid their detailed plans for the defeat of Japan before me for approval. There had apparently been some differences of opinion as to the best route to be followed, but these had evidently been reconciled, for when General Marshall had presented his plan for a two-phase invasion of Japan, Admiral King and General Arnold had supported the proposal heartily.

The Army plan envisaged an amphibious landing in the fall of 1945 on the island of Kyushu, the southernmost of the Japanese home islands. This would be accomplished by our Sixth Army, under the command of General Walter Krueger. The first landing would then be followed approximately four months later by a second great invasion, which would be carried out by our Eighth and Tenth Armies, followed by the First Army transferred from Europe, all of which would go ashore in the Kanto plains area near Tokyo. In all, it had been estimated that it would require until the late fall of 1946 to bring Japan to her knees.

This was a formidable conception, and all of us realized fully that the fighting would be fierce and the losses heavy. But it was hoped that some of Japan's forces would continue to be preoccupied in China and others would be prevented from reinforcing the home islands if Russia were to enter the war.

There was, of course, always the possibility that the Japanese might choose to surrender sooner. Our air and fleet units had begun to inflict heavy damage on industrial and urban sites in Japan proper. Except in China, the armies of the Mikado had been pushed back everywhere in relentless successions of defeats.

Acting Secretary of State Grew had spoken to me in late May about issuing a proclamation that would urge the Japanese to surrender but would assure them that we would permit the Emperor to remain as head of the state. Grew backed this with arguments taken from his ten years' experience as our Ambassador in Japan, and I told him that I had already given thought to this matter myself and that it seemed to me a sound idea. Grew had a draft of a proclamation with him, and I instructed him to send it by the customary channels to the Joint Chiefs and the State-War-Navy Co-ordinating Committee in order that we might get the opinions of all concerned before I made my decision.

On June 18 Grew reported that the proposal had met with the approval of his Cabinet colleagues and of the Joint Chiefs. The military leaders also discussed the subject with me when they reported the same day. Grew, however, favored issuing the proclamation at once, to coincide with the closing of the campaign on Okinawa, while the service chiefs were of the opinion that we should wait until we were ready to follow a Japanese refusal with the actual assault of our invasion forces.

Developing the Bomb

It was my decision then that the proclamation to Japan should be issued from the forthcoming conference at Potsdam. This, I believed, would clearly demonstrate to Japan and to the world that the Allies were united in their purpose. By that time, also, we might know more about two matters of significance for our future effort: the participation of the Soviet Union and the atomic bomb. We knew that the bomb would receive its first test in mid-July. If the test of the bomb was successful, I wanted to afford Japan a clear chance to end the fighting before we made use of this newly gained power. If the test should fail, then it would be even more important to us to bring about a surrender before we had to make a physical conquest of Japan. General Marshall told me that it might cost half a million American lives to force the enemy's surrender on his home grounds.

But the test was now successful. The entire development of the atomic bomb had been dictated by military considerations. The idea of the atomic bomb had been suggested to President Roosevelt by the famous and brilliant Dr. Albert Einstein, and its development turned out to be a vast undertaking. It was the achievement of the combined efforts of science, industry, labor, and the military, and it had no parallel in history. The men in charge and their staffs worked under extremely high pressure, and the whole enormous task required the services of more than one hundred thousand men and immense quantities of material. It required over two and a half years and necessitated the expenditure of two and a half billions of dollars.

Only a handful of the thousands of men who worked in these plants knew what they were producing. So strict was the secrecy imposed that even some of the highest-ranking officials in Washington had not the slightest idea of what was going on. I did not. Before 1939 it had been generally agreed among scientists that it was theoretically possible to release energy from the atom. In 1940 we had begun to pool with Great Britain all scientific knowledge useful to war, although Britain was at war at that time and we were not. Following this—in 1942—we learned that the Germans were at work on a method to harness atomic energy for use as a weapon of war. This, we understood, was to be added to the V-1 and V-2 rockets with which they hoped to conquer the world. They failed, of course, and for this we can thank Providence. But now a race was on to make the atomic bomb—a race that became "the battle of the laboratories."

It was under the general policy of pooling knowledge between our nation and Great Britain that research on the atomic bomb started in such feverish secrecy. American and British scientists joined in the race against the Germans. We in America had available a great number of distinguished scientists in many related fields of knowledge, and we also had another great advantage. We could provide the tremendous industrial and economic resources required for the project—a vastly expensive project—without injury to our war production program. Furthermore, our plants were far removed from the reach of enemy bombing. Britain, whose scientists had initiated the project and were contributing much of the original atomic data, was constantly exposed to enemy bombing and, when she started the atomic research, also faced the possibility of invasion.

For these reasons Roosevelt and Churchill agreed to pool the research and concentrate all of the work on the development of the project within the United States. Working together with the British, we thus made it possible to achieve a great scientific triumph in the field of atomic energy. Nevertheless, basic and historic as this event was, it had to be considered at the time as relatively incidental to the far-flung war we were fighting in the Pacific at terrible cost in American lives.

We could hope for a miracle, but the daily tragedy of a bitter war crowded in on us. We labored to construct a weapon of such overpowering force that the enemy could be forced to yield swiftly once we could resort to it. This was the primary aim of our secret and vast effort. But we also had to carry out the enormous effort of our basic and traditional military plans.

The task of creating the atomic bomb had been entrusted to a special unit of the Army Corps of Engineers, the so-called Manhattan District, headed by Major General Leslie R. Groves. The primary effort, however, had come from British and American scientists working in laboratories and offices scattered throughout the nation.

Dr. J. Robert Oppenheimer, the distinguished physicist from the University of California, had set up the key establishment in the whole process at Los Alamos, New Mexico. More than any other one man, Oppenheimer is to be credited with the achievement of the completed bomb.

The President's Committee

My own knowledge of these developments had come about only after I became President, when Secretary Stimson had given me the full story. He had told me at that time that the project was nearing completion and that a bomb could be expected within another four months. It was at his suggestion, too, that I had then set up a committee of top men and had asked them to study with great care the implications the new weapon might have for us.

Secretary Stimson headed this group as chairman, and the other members were George L. Harrison, president of the New York Life Insurance Company, who was then serving as a special assistant to the Secretary of War; James F. Byrnes, as my personal representative; Ralph A. Bard, Under Secretary of the Navy; Assistant Secretary William L. Clayton for the State Department; and three of our most renowned scientists—Dr. Vannevar Bush, president of the Carnegie Institution of Washington and Director of the Office of Scientific Research and Development; Dr. Karl T. Compton, president of the Massachusetts Institute of Technology and Chief of Field Service in the Office of Scientific Research and Development; and Dr. James B. Conant, president of Harvard University and chairman of the National Defense Research Committee.

This committee was assisted by a group of scientists, of whom those most prominently connected with the development of the atomic bomb were Dr. Oppenheimer, Dr. Arthur H. Compton, Dr. E.O. Lawrence, and the Italian-born Dr. Enrico Fermi. The conclusions reached by these men, both in the advisory committee of scientists and in the larger committee, were brought to me by Secretary Stimson on June 1.

It was their recommendation that the bomb be used against the enemy as soon as it could be done. They recommended further that it should be used without specific warning and against a target that would clearly show its devastating strength. I had realized, of course, that an atomic bomb explosion would inflict damage and casualties beyond imagination. On the other hand, the scientific advisers of the committee reported, "We can propose no technical demonstration likely to bring an end to the war; we see no acceptable alternative to direct military use." It was their conclusion that no technical demonstration they might propose, such as over a deserted island, would be likely to bring the war to an end. It had to be used against an enemy target.

The final decision of where and when to use the atomic bomb was up to me. Let there be no mistake about it. I regarded the bomb as a military weapon and never had any doubt that it should be used. The top military advisers to the President recommended its use, and when I talked to Churchill he unhesitatingly told me that he favored the use of the atomic bomb if it might aid to end the war.

Orders to Drop the Bomb

In deciding to use this bomb I wanted to make sure that it would be used as a weapon of war in the manner prescribed by the laws of war. That meant that I wanted it dropped on a military target. I had told Stimson that the bomb should be dropped as nearly as possibly upon a war production center of prime military importance.

Stimson's staff had prepared a list of cities in Japan that might serve as targets. Kyoto, though favored by General Arnold as a center of military activity, was eliminated when Secretary Stimson pointed out that it was a cultural and religious shrine of the Japanese.

Four cities were finally recommended as targets: Hiroshima, Kokura, Niigata, and Nagasaki. They were listed in that order as targets for the first attack. The order of selection was in accordance with the military importance of these cities, but allowance would be given for weather conditions at the time of the bombing. Before the selected targets were approved as proper for military purposes, I personally went over them in detail with Stimson, Marshall, and Arnold, and we discussed the matter of timing and the final choice of the first target.

General Spaatz, who commanded the Strategic Air Forces, which would deliver the bomb on the target, was given some latitude as to when and on which of the four targets the bomb would be dropped. That was necessary because of weather and other operational considerations. In order to get preparations under way, the War Department was given orders to instruct General Spaatz that the first bomb would be dropped as soon after August 3 as weather would permit. The order to General Spaatz read as follows:

24 July 1945

TO: General Carl Spaatz
  Commanding General
  United States Army Strategic Air Forces

1. The 509 Composite Group, 20th Air Force will deliver its first special bomb as soon as weather will permit visual bombing after about 3 August 1945 on one of the targets: Hiroshima, Kokura, Niigata and Nagasaki. To carry military and civilian scientific personnel from the War Department to observe and record the effects of the explosion of the bomb, additional aircraft will accompany the airplane carrying the bomb. The observing planes will stay several miles distant from the point of impact of the bomb.

2. Additional bombs will be delivered on the above targets as soon as made ready by the project staff. Further instructions will be issued concerning targets other than those listed above.

3. Dissemination of any and all information concerning the use of the weapon against Japan is reserved to the Secretary of War and the President of the United States. No communique on the subject or release of information will be issued by Commanders in the field without specific prior authority. Any news stories will be sent to the War Department for special clearance.

4. The foregoing directive is issued to you by direction and with the approval of the Secretary of War and the Chief of Staff, U.S.A. It is desired that you personally deliver one copy of this directive to General MacArthur and one copy to Admiral Nimitz for their information.

/s/ Thos. T. Handy
General, GSC
Acting Chief of Staff

With this order the wheels were set in motion for the first use of an atomic weapon against a military target. I had made the decision. I also instructed Stimson that the order would stand unless I notified him that the Japanese reply to our ultimatum was acceptable.

A specialized B-29 unit, known as the 509th Composite Group, had been selected for the task, and seven of the modified B-29's, with pilots and crews, were ready and waiting for orders. Meanwhile ships and planes were rushing the materials for the bomb and specialists to assemble them to the Pacific island of Tinian in the Marianas.

On July 28 Radio Tokyo announced that the Japanese government would continue to fight. There was no formal reply to the joint ultimatum of the United States, the United Kingdom, and China. There was no alternative now. The bomb was scheduled to be dropped after August 3 unless Japan surrendered before that day.

"News That Shook the World"

On August 6, the fourth day of the journey home from Potsdam, came the historic news that shook the world. I was eating lunch with members of the *Augusta*'s crew when Captain Frank Graham, White House Map Room watch officer, handed me the following message:

> TO THE PRESIDENT
>
> FROM THE SECRETARY OF WAR
>
> Big bomb dropped on Hiroshima August 5 at 7:15 P.M. Washington time. First reports indicate complete success which was even more conspicuous than earlier test.

I was greatly moved. I telephoned Byrnes aboard ship to give him the news and then said to the group of sailors around me, "This is the greatest thing in history. It's time for us to get home."

A few minutes later a second message was handed to me. It read as follows:

> Following info regarding Manhattan received. "Hiroshima

bombed visually with only one tenth cover at 052315A. There was no fighter opposition and no flak. Parsons reports 15 minutes after drop as follows: 'Results clear cut successful in all respects. Visible effects greater than in any test. Conditions normal in airplane following delivery.'"

When I had read this I signaled to the crew in the mess hall that I wished to say something. I then told them of the dropping of a powerful new bomb which used an explosive twenty thousand times as powerful as a ton of TNT. I went to the wardroom, where I told the officers, who were at lunch, what had happened. I could not keep back my expectation that the Pacific war might now be brought to a speedy end.

A few minutes later the ship's radio receivers began to carry news bulletins from Washington about the atomic bomb, as well as a broadcast of the statement I had authorized just before leaving Germany. Shortly afterward I called a press conference of the correspondents on board and told them something of the long program of research and development that lay behind this successful assault.

Truman's Statement on the Atomic Bomb

My statements on the atomic bomb, which had been released in Washington by Stimson, read in part as follows:

"... But the greatest marvel is not the size of the enterprise, its secrecy, nor its cost, but the achievement of scientific brains in putting together infinitely complex pieces of knowledge held by many men in different fields of science into a workable plan. And hardly less marvelous has been the capacity of industry to design, and of labor to operate, the machines and methods to do things never done before, so that the brain child of many minds came forth in physical shape and performed as it was supposed to do. Both science and industry worked under the direction of the United States Army, which achieved a unique success in managing so diverse a problem in the advancement of knowledge in an amazingly short time. It is doubtful if such another combination could be got together in the world. What has been done is the greatest achievement of organized science in history. It was done under high pressure and without failure.

"We are now prepared to obliterate more rapidly and completely every productive enterprise the Japanese have above ground in any city. We shall destroy their docks, their factories, and their communications. Let there be no mistake; we shall completely destroy Japan's power to make war.

"It was to spare the Japanese people from utter destruction that the ultimatum of July 26 was issued at Potsdam. Their leaders promptly rejected that ultimatum. If they do not now accept our terms, they may expect a rain of ruin from the air, the like of which has never been seen on this earth. Behind this air attack will follow sea and land forces in such numbers and power as they have not yet seen and with the fighting skill of which they are already well aware.

". . . The fact that we can release atomic energy ushers in a new era in man's understanding of nature's forces. Atomic energy may in the future supplement the power that now comes from coal, oil, and falling water, but at present it cannot be produced on a basis to compete with them commercially. Before that comes there must be a long period of intensive research.

"It has never been the habit of the scientists of this country or the policy of this Government to withhold from the world scientific knowledge. Normally, therefore, everything about the work with atomic energy would be made public.

"But under present circumstances it is not intended to divulge the technical processes of production or all the military applications, pending further examination of possible methods of protecting us and the rest of the world from the danger of sudden destruction.

"I shall recommend that the Congress of the United States consider promptly the establishment of an appropriate commission to control the production and use of atomic power within the United States.

"I shall give further consideration and make further recommendations to the Congress as to how atomic power can become a powerful and forceful influence towards the maintenance of world peace."

Still no surrender offer came. An order was issued to General Spaatz to continue operations as planned unless otherwise instructed. . . .

Nagasaki and Surrender

On August 9 the second atom bomb was dropped, this time on Nagasaki. We gave the Japanese three days in which to make up their minds to surrender, and the bombing would have been held off another two days had weather permitted. During those three days we indicated that we meant business. On August 7 the 20th Air Force sent out a bomber force of some one hundred and thirty B-29's, and on the eighth it reported four hundred and twenty B-29's in day and night attacks. The choice of targets for the second atom bomb was first Kokura, with Nagasaki second. The third city on the list, Niigata, had been ruled out as too distant. By the time Kokura was reached the weather had closed in, and after three runs over the spot without a glimpse of the target, with gas running short, a try was made for the second choice, Nagasaki. There, too, the weather had closed in, but an opening in the clouds gave the bombardier his chance, and Nagasaki was successfully bombed.

This second demonstration of the power of the atomic bomb apparently threw Tokyo into a panic, for the next morning brought the first indication that the Japanese Empire was ready to surrender.

Chapter 4

The Aftermath

Chapter Preface

According to a Japanese survivor of the August 6, 1945, Hiroshima bombing, Agawa Hiroyuki, "the dead excluding soldiers were 59,000 to 64,000 in mid-December that year . . . 50 percent dying during the first six days, and 99 percent during the first forty days." Later estimates would put the total loss of life at 140,000. A second bomb was dropped on Nagasaki on August 9. The blast of the "Fat Man" plutonium bomb was almost twice the power of the Hiroshima bomb. Forty thousand people were instantly annihilated. The city was 90 percent destroyed. Faced with such devastation, Japan surrendered on August 10, ending World War II.

After the war, the Manhattan Project was officially terminated. Los Alamos continued its research and development of nuclear weapons, but both the military and peaceful use of nuclear energy was handed over to the civilian-controlled Atomic Energy Commission on January 1, 1947. During the years just after World War II, many scientists and politicians hoped that nuclear energy could be developed into a cheap and plentiful source of power that would benefit all human kind. They also wanted to deter the destructive potential of nuclear weapons through international regulation. In his "Atoms for Peace" speech before the United Nations on December 8, 1953, President Eisenhower proposed that the United States and the Soviet Union "begin now and continue to make joint contributions from their stockpiles of normal uranium and fissionable materials to an international atomic energy agency." This dream of an "international atomic energy agency" was shattered when Russia rejected the United States' proposal to the United Nations. Russia was just beginning to develop its own atomic bombs and it was not willing to give up their nuclear weapons program. The Russians began testing their nuclear weapons in 1949, and the United

States, despite opposition by scientists such as Oppenheimer and Fermi, developed the super bomb or hydrogen bomb—thousands of times more powerful than the bomb dropped on Hiroshima. The first U.S. hydrogen bomb test was in November 1952. The Soviets followed with their own hydrogen bomb test in August 1953. The arms race predicted in 1945 by physicists Leo Szilard, James Franck, and Glen Seaborg was now in full swing. The race would not slow until the Strategic Arms Limitations agreements between the United States and Russia in the 1970s.

Despite the peaceful uses of nuclear energy and the nuclear arms limitations agreements between the nations possessing nuclear weapons, the United States is still struggling to solve what Eisenhower called "the fearful atomic dilemma . . . to find the way by which the miraculous inventiveness of man shall not be dedicated to his death, but consecrated to his life."

Surviving the Hiroshima Blast

Agawa Hiroyuki and Kazuko Hiroyuki

In this account written two years after the atom bomb
exploded over Hiroshima, a father and daughter share their
remembrances of surviving the horrific event. The father,
Agawa Hiroyuki, was working at city hall when the blast
came on August 6, 1945. The shock knocked him unconscious for some time. He awoke in a daze but soon focused
his attention on finding his daughter, a student who worked at
the Postal Savings Bureau, a short distance from city hall.
Unable to locate her and worried about his wife and parents,
he struggled through the devastated city toward his home. As
he walked the streets, he crossed several districts of the city—
Danbara, Iwahana, Onaga, and into the Nakayama Pass—trying to find his way to Hakushima, his home on the outskirts
of the city. On his journey, he witnessed the terrible injuries
of other survivors and the utter destruction of the city.

Kazuko, Agawa Hiroyuki's daughter, then begins her tale.
She was lucky enough not to go straight to work that day. The
bomb hit as she was riding the streetcar and she miraculously
escaped injury. She wandered the city trying to get home and
seeing the terrible effects of the blast. The next day she found
her mother sitting in a field near their home, and soon her
father also appeared. Kazuko developed symptoms of radiation sickness, but she gradually recovered. The father suffered
many ailments of "atomic disease" for over a year until he
finally recovered. Their stories are collected with other

Excerpted from "The Father's Note," by Agawa Hiroyuki and Kazuko Hiroyuki, *The
Atomic Bomb: Voices from Hiroshima and Nagasaki*, edited by Kyoko Selden and Mark
Selden (Armonk, NY: M.E. Sharpe Inc., 1989). Copyright © 1989 by M.E. Sharpe Inc.
Reprinted with permission.

Hiroshima and Nagasaki survivors in *The Atomic Bomb: Voices from Hiroshima and Nagasaki.*

The second anniversary of those who died from the atomic bomb approaches. Memories of the nightmare are gradually fading. I would like to record my family's experiences at that time.

My family was then six people: my parents, myself, my wife, and a son and daughter. I was fifty-four. Of these, only my father died, . . . the other five survived, having gone through different experiences in different places. My son, however, did not directly encounter the bomb. . . .

Until then I had worked at xx section in the Hiroshima City Government. On August 6, I went to City Hall somewhat earlier than usual, entered xx section on the southeast side of the third floor, and, facing east at my desk in the center of the room, was making a chart needed in my work. Then, suddenly, I heard a strange sound which had great depth. It sounded like "packkoon." As I looked to my left (north), puzzled, my eyes caught a white, egg-shell-color light, and I thought, oh no, a direct hit above our heads; instantly I felt as though the entire ferro-concrete City Hall swayed, and I lost consciousness.

I do not know how many minutes I was unconscious; anyway, after a while I became aware, as if in a dream, of my own groaning and of thick smoke, and while thinking and thinking that something was wrong, I came to my senses. I felt as if I was bathing in grease. Looking at myself I found that blood was streaming all over my body. The bleeding was worst around the left wrist and head; blood was also flowing from the shoulders to the chest. I looked around the room, my eyes wide open. Until just a moment ago I was sure there had been six people, but now I was the only one left, and, as if toy boxes were turned over and pushed to one side of the room, chairs, desks and document shelves were blown off to the side in a great mess. I, too, had been blown there. Smoke streamed in through the door. Collecting myself, I rose. Since my legs were somewhat wobbly, I went out to the hallway holding onto something. I heard low groans from different directions; I looked around, however, to find the building apparently intact. Concerned about my bike, which I had left in the janitor's room with important registration papers strapped to it, I started down the stairs.

On the way down, a woman of about forty (so I thought but she might have been younger) was dead, her mouth, like a wolf's, torn from ear to ear and both eyeballs blown out. It hardly looked like a human face. When I went down to the second floor, I saw several more such people. My feet refusing to move, I stopped and looked down at the courtyard from a second floor window. In the courtyard below, thick yellow smoke was hanging at human height, and above it was a mass of jet black smoke. From the public hall next door a rather thin stream of smoke was approaching. When I saw this, for the first time I felt that some new weapon might have been used.

Then, too, I saw an odd sight through the smoke. Many office girls were walking in a circle in the courtyard, raising their hands as they would in a Bon dance. Half of them were barefooted, and they were all calling: "Mother, please come." "Mother, why aren't you coming?"

Their voices were sad screams that resembled sobbing, in an indescribably pitiful, disagreeable tone. The moment someone diverged, the odd Bon dance circle went out of shape in that direction. And, while becoming now circular and now oblong, it was going round and round in the same way. They seemed like human beings who had lost all reason. Although in retrospect all might have been able to flee if someone reliable had skillfully guided them, beneath my eyes about ten fell one after another.

I no longer cared about my bike. I ran from the south stairs in the center to the streetcar road. My legs became firmer, though probably only from terror. On the street, electric poles lay on one side like fallen incense sticks. A horse-drawn wagon carrying metal pipes had tumbled and lay on its side, both horse and man having died instantly. I started to walk a little northward, but, frightened by high-voltage electric sparks, I retreated and passed through the west gate of the College of Arts and Sciences in the direction of the Red Cross Hospital. On the campus, where there were as yet no flames, I saw five or six men, probably teachers, talking with few words as though all spirit had gone out of them.

Searching for His Daughter

I was worried about my home in Hakushima, but at that point what worried me even more was what had happened to my daughter, who should have been working at the Postal Savings Bureau right near where I was. Passing before the Red Cross Hospital, I looked up at the reddish building. She worked there every day due to student labor mobilization. That morning, she should have left home slightly later than I. With painful thoughts, I paced up and down in front of the building. Injured people flowed into this wide street from different places and all walked toward Ujina. There was also a naked woman who, although not wounded, ran barefooted muttering something unintelligible, her hair in disarray. I grabbed many people to inquire, but none knew about the Savings Bureau. After a while an old man told me, "At the Savings Bureau, they dragged seriously injured people down to the basement."

Approaching the basement entrance, I saw two guard-like men with pickaxes barking, "We'll kill anyone who goes in here." Since my nerves were on edge, however, I tried to break in, paying no attention. One of them blocked me, brandishing his pickaxe: "How dare you break in here?"

"What? Kill me if you like. My precious daughter was drafted for forced labor service: What's wrong about her parent entering to search at such a time? Go ahead, kill me if you can," I yelled loudly. I must have glared at him with a terribly threatening expression. Cowed, the man put down his pickaxe and let me pass.

Compared with the tumult outside, the basement was gloomy and subdued. I heard low groans here and there.

"Kazuko, Kazuko," I called my daughter's name, my

voice resounding in the basement. I walked around, peering at one face after another of the seriously wounded people. Among them were a few young women. Once, I stepped on something soft and limp and jumped back startled. It was a human hand. It belonged to a lean man of about thirty, seemingly already dead.

"Ojisan, ojisan" (sir, sir), a boy called in a low voice, holding out both hands as though asking for help.

"Keep up your spirits. Someone will come soon."

Holding his hands, I think I said something like this. I myself could do nothing for him. I just went outside. I could not find my daughter. Although I went outside, I could not give her up. While gauging the flames visible in all directions near and far and the possibilities of escape, I wandered this way and that, hatless under the scorching sun, until I think it was about eleven. No matter who I asked, no one responded in earnest. Finally giving up, I started to flee, following the lines of people. When I came as far as the Miyuki Bridge and looked from our neighborhood toward Ushita, I saw smoke rising from the shadows of the Ushita mountains. The mountains seemed to have caught fire.

Trying to Reach Home

From this point on, my memory is somewhat hazy.

Where was it?—I seem to think it was on the river bank.

I ran through something like an army dump and a split second later fire from across the street licked the whole building.

Around Danbara, everyone I saw told me about what lay ahead. I was trying somehow to reach home.

"It's no use. Even if you went further, you'd just be burnt to death. Every place is a sea of fire," some said, while others said, "The fire isn't as bad as you think. Cheer up."

Then, somewhere, four trucks, I think of the army, were busily working at moving seriously injured people. I was urged to get on. When I asked their destination, I was told that they were taking the injured to Kaita-ichi and Ujina. It was the wrong direction, so I continued to walk on.

When I put together what various people had said, it seemed that I could get to Ushita if I bypassed Hiroshima Station, went through Iwahana, and crossed Nakayama Pass beyond the east parade ground, so I set out intending to do that. If I reached Ushita, I could return to Hakushima, or, even if I failed, I thought I would be able to get some information about my family. When passing Onaga, where the damage was relatively light, someone said, "Sir, you are bleeding heavily. I don't know how far you're going, but why don't you stay here for the night?"

Although I felt grateful, I declined that offer, too.

Soon I came to the pass. By then I keenly felt the pain from my wounds, and my legs were heavy as though there were metal rods in them; it wasn't easy to climb the trail at the pass.

I looked back, resting on the roots of a tree. The entire city was engulfed in black smoke, and although it was still early, the feel of evening dusk hung everywhere, the sun only faintly visible. Beneath my eyes, only the flames on Hiroshima Station were bright red.

Passing seriously injured people lying on both sides of the pass, I walked a little and rested, rested and climbed again. When finally I could no longer walk, I crawled to a hut I happened to find. Peering inside, I saw several soldiers, who invited me in. Among the soldiers was an army captain, who looked like a doctor, accompanied by a woman of about thirty-four or thirty-five. He prepared strong sugar water to revive me. After I drank two cups, my body was suddenly invigorated and I felt elated. I also received from him two green tomatoes and nibbled at them. He gave me no treatment; probably he had nothing to treat my wounds with.

I rose after staying there a while, thanked them, and started to walk again. Now and then I met people coming from the opposite direction. I was the only one walking toward Ushita. A young man passing by tried to stop me: "Don't be a fool, ojisan. Why are you going there? Everyone's fleeing from there. Don't be a fool."

But I shook him off, too. The sugar water had only revived

me momentarily: fatigue permeated my entire body. I was walking, half-awake, half-asleep, thinking that the house was no longer there and both my parents and my wife had died. In time big sparks started to fly toward me one after another, and at that point I met another person, a woman of about fifty, appearing from the opposite direction. From this old woman I heard that Ushita had not burnt, that Hakushima was slow in catching fire, and that many Hakushima people survived, having fled to Ushita. While listening, I felt my legs become light and fell on the grass, losing consciousness.

The Daughter's Story

A fourth-year student at the Second Prefectural Girls' School of Hiroshima, I had been mobilized to work at the Savings Bureau. On the morning of the 6th the alarm sounded, so I waited for the all clear and then left home. When I came to the Hakushima terminal, a streetcar was just about to leave. It wasn't that we had a special promise, but since I always met my friend Yasuko there and went to work with her on the same streetcar, I hesitated a little when I didn't see her, wondering if I should wait for another car. However, I was somewhat late that day and, moreover, the car was conveniently bound for Dentetsu Station (a car bound for Dentetsu Station spared me the trouble of changing at Hatcho-bori), so I made up my mind and got on. Around the time when the streetcar passed Kamiya, I recalled that I had left at school the book *How to Grow Vegetables at Home* which I had promised to lend to the section head a few days earlier. Again I hesitated whether to go to the bank or stay on as far as school to get the book. I decided to go to school first. Besides the book, there was something I wanted to see Teacher S about. I hesitated twice; I don't know what would have happened to me had I acted differently on even one of these two occasions.

"A Terrible Blue Light"

Past the Red Cross Hospital, past the Savings Bureau, when the streetcar ran a little further, a terrible blue light flashed, spreading as far as I could see. Instantly I thought that the streetcar had had an accident, and I reflected: what a mistake, after all I shouldn't have taken this car. In fact, of course, it was just the opposite: although the details are unknown, Yasuko seems to have come from the Hakushima terminal to Hatcho-bori on the next car, and while waiting to transfer there she was hit by that light and, seriously wounded, just managed to run home. She died the next day. Well, the car I rode stopped right away and its passengers noisily got off. As I, too, got off and stood on the street, the world was all dark, visited at that moment by an eerie hush. Forgetting myself, I shouted loudly, "I can't see, I can't see."

The hush, however, lasted just for a second, and soon howls rose everywhere. Voices calling for help, cries complaining of pain, groans—while I was wondering what could have happened, little by little the darkness wore off and changed to a dawn-like color around me. As I looked in that light, those wearing army caps were intact only under their caps; the rest of their facial skin had peeled off in big pieces like loquat peels and was hanging from cheeks and necks. The skin on their hands had also come off. Many people dangled both hands in front of their chests ghostlike, everyone in the same way, the skin hanging. They aimlessly paced this way and that. Their faces and arms where the skin had slid off looked pink. This pink was truly chilling, and, although my father says it is better to avoid exaggeration, I really thought this was hell. I myself seemed without injury of any kind. That day my outfit was navy blue work pants, a half-sleeve gym shirt, and on my feet a pair of clogs. How I had escaped wounds anywhere on my body puzzles me even now. When I noticed, I had only one clog on. I had left the other in the streetcar. When I looked at people wandering left and right, at least everyone had clogs on both feet. Suddenly embarrassed, I thought of going back to the streetcar for my other clog. Putting a foot on the step, I found that the floor of the car had collapsed, and it was in such a mess that I could not get in. I seem to remember that the car was burning, but it may just be that it had broken down. Giving up the clog, I started to run.

Fleeing the City

After that, I don't remember how I ran, or what road I took. I think I probably didn't pass the Savings Bureau. I remember standing helplessly for a while in front of City Hall, worried about my father. Since my body was fine, many people called out to me "help me, help me." This made me feel helpless. A bloody man lying on the road called for help; an old woman also called, only her hands and face visible beneath a flattened zinc roof. Each time I fled, pretending to close my eyes and covering my ears. I met people coming from the opposite direction spreading rumors that the bridge ahead had burnt down and that oil had been poured into the river, turning it into a river of fire. I wondered what I should do; but such rumors were all lies. When I came to the bridge, an army officer was talking loudly with someone in a boat moored to the bank. Since the boat started drifting upstream propelled by the wind the moment he tried to untie the cord, he seemed preoccupied with doing something about it. Someone questioned the officer: "Sir, what on earth happened today?"

The officer, a young man with the rank of lieutenant, answered, "It seems that the enemy dropped air torpedoes."

Since my brother was in the navy, I had heard that air torpedoes were dropped from airplanes against enemy ships; I thought the answer strange, but thinking at that moment that he might be right, I started to run again. When I had run for quite a while, a young man a little over twenty called to me, "Say, wait a second."

When I stopped, he said, "It's dangerous to cross the bridge the way you are. Let me give you this."

He took off his army sock and handed it to me. I realized that I was running with one clog on. Then, for the first time, I clearly knew where I was. I was about to cross Yokogawa Bridge. There, I dusted dirt off the foot without a clog, wore the sock the young man offered me, and crossed the bridge as he pulled my hand. Although a little blood somehow smudged the foot without a clog, I wasn't injured much.

From then on I walked with him. A while later, a man of about fifty years old also joined, and the three of us ran side by side.

Black Rain

Soon after we three got together, it suddenly started to rain hard. The rain was as black as heavy oil, and my clothes became wet black. When I took a careful look, they were— since when I didn't know—spotted with blood here and there. It was not my blood; I think injured people's blood splattered. The young man said, "Let's go, let's go. Whether rain falls or spears fall, it's all the same now."

Besides, there was no place for sheltering against the rain. We three kept on walking, drenched. The man about fifty also said, "Anyway it's better to get out and away from Hiroshima as quickly as possible." Somehow unable to mention that my house was in Hakushima, I followed the two men like someone without will. The fiftyish man, we learned, had been fishing near Misasa Bridge. When he chanced to look up, he saw three round shining objects fall side by side, and he barely had time to wonder about them before he was blown to the center of the river by the boom. His partially dry clothes became wet again in the rain. His left arm was badly injured.

We had walked along the right bank of the Ota River quite a distance from Hiroshima City when the rain stopped. Since there happened to be a boat on the river bank, I decided to ask the boatman to ferry me to the opposite bank so I could go home, and I parted with the two men. The opposite bank was the northern limit of Ushita. This time I headed south and reached the house of my friend Miss Kimura. I meant to leave after a little rest to look for my parents and grandparents, but I was forced to stay. "Right now fire seems to be raging in Hakushima, so we can't let you go; wait a little longer," they said. After all I stayed at my friend's house for the night. About that time, people in the neighborhood were panicking, saying that the air raid alarm had gone off again.

Finding Mother and Father

That night I slept poorly due to fear and worry. Early the following morning I tried to find the ruins of my house in Hakushima. The town was completely burnt, but I found my mother and grandmother absentmindedly sitting with neighbors in a field near the river. Recognizing me, mother rose reeling and said, "Oh, Kazu-chan."

Unable to say anything, I went down with a thump on my knees as though in prayer. Soon my father returned with terrible injuries. Although I learned that my grandfather had died, I was not at all sad then. Much later, when a shed was built and we had a monk recite sutras, then for the first time I cried aloud.

As I have written earlier, I was uninjured, but a little later the so-called atomic disease symptoms appeared: spots broke out here and there on my skin, my body felt dull, I had a fever, I lost appetite. For a long time I commuted to the hospital with my father and mother. When I was tested, the number of white cells had gone down to the 1,900s. I learned that the normal figure is about 7,000. At one point I thought I was dying, but since late fall I gradually recovered, and now I am fine. . .

The Father's Postscript

The above is a composite record of that day. . . . On rereading it, I cannot help feeling exasperated: unless we add much, much more, we will not really convey to the reader the events of the day. Indeed, our experiences were such that one who did not see that day could never imagine them however he tried.

From around the time my external wounds finally healed in November, I started to be afflicted by diarrhea of unknown cause. I visited every doctor I could find and tried every possible treatment, such as taking plum puree I obtained from someone in Kyoto, a traditional family medicine in Wakayama. Around the time the year changed, however, it only grew worse and worse. My stomach grumbled like a musical band, and everything passed through even though I felt no pain and enjoyed meals. For this reason I became nearly skin and bones and wondered whether I would die of this diarrhea after having luckily survived. Hearing around that time of Dr. T who had come from Tokyo for research, I visited him and found as many as eleven patients with the same symptoms as mine squeezing into his office. Told that this was a kind of atomic disease, I followed his directions to take as much bone marrow as possible: preparing myself to enter into a life like that of a wild dog, I bit into all the bones I saw, whether sardine or chicken. Perhaps it had some effect, for a year later the tenacious diarrhea finally stopped, and my body began to recover daily. Later, I had a chance to see Dr. T's research notes. According to the beginning portion of his notes, the estimated Hiroshima City population at the time of the bombing was 230,000 to 260,000; the dead excluding soldiers were 59,000 to 64,000 in mid-December that year; and the number of the dead decreased in the manner of a geometric progression from the day of the bombing, 50 percent dying during the first six days, and 99 percent during the first forty days. The bombing occurred at 8:15 A.M. on August 6, 1945.

Surveying the Damage to Nagasaki and Hiroshima

Kenneth D. Nichols and Stafford L. Warren

Major General Kenneth D. Nichols, one of the top-level commanders of the Manhattan Project, recounts the events just before and after the Japanese surrender. He states that even after the second bomb was dropped on Nagasaki on August 9, 1945, Nichols's superior, Brigadier General Groves, ordered the Manhattan Project to prepare a third bomb to be used against the Japanese homeland. But within days, the Japanese did surrender, and the U.S. military turned their attention to learning the specific effects these bombs had on people and the environment of the two devastated cities.

Nichols sent various groups to Japan to assess the damage. One of these groups was a survey team under Stafford L. Warren. They left San Francisco, California, on August 14, 1945, and surveyed Hiroshima on September 8 and Nagasaki on October 8. Warren found radioactive contamination to be lower than had been expected. His report also evaluated the effects of the atomic blasts on buildings and the human body. The survey documented burns, internal injuries, anemia, purpura (small lesions and bruises on the skin), epilation (loss of hair), and low white blood cell count as the main ailments of the surviving victims.

After the quoted report by Warren, Nichols resumes his account, revealing what the Americans knew about the effects

Excerpted from *The Road To Trinity*, by Kenneth D. Nichols (New York: William Morrow and Company Inc., 1987). Copyright © 1987 by Kenneth D. Nichols. Reprinted by permission of the publisher.

of radiation before the bombs were dropped. He states that they tried to minimize radiation by detonating the bombs high enough in the atmosphere to dissipate much of the radioactivity. They did this mainly to protect American troops that would soon occupy the defeated Japanese cities. Warren's survey and additional studies found no increase in genetic defects and no irreversible environmental damage from radiation. Nichols acknowledges that there is much dispute over these studies, and the controversy continues to the present day. But he says that additional studies will never change "the horrible effect of nuclear or thermonuclear war." However, Nichols believes that the two bombs dropped on Japan ultimately saved lives and ended the war. This account is taken from Nichols's 1987 memoir, *The Road to Trinity*.

E ven after we had dropped the plutonium bomb on Nagasaki, we received no immediate indication that Japan would accept our peace terms. . . . Groves sent the following memo to General Marshall on August 10: "The next bomb of the implosion type had been scheduled to be ready for delivery on the target on the first good weather after 24 August 1945. We have gained 4 days in manufacture and expect to ship from New Mexico on 12 or 13 August the final components. Providing there are no unforeseen difficulties in manufacture, in transportation to the theatre or after arrival in the theatre, the bomb should be ready for delivery on the first suitable weather after 17 or 18 August."

Anticipating Japanese acceptance of peace terms, Marshall wrote on the memo: "It is not to be released over Japan without express authority from the President." On the thirteenth, Groves sent a memo to General Handy that he would remind him on Wednesday, the fifteenth, "that I am ready to start shipment. I will arrange for planes so that they can depart from New Mexico on Thursday if the decision is to send the materials. This will change date in theatre from (subject to first good weather) the 20th or 21st." Meanwhile, Los Alamos was preparing for their next shipment. On the fourteenth, with a car waiting outside, Dr. Robert Bacher [head of experimental physics at Los Alamos] was in the ice house completing the packaging of the core for the third bomb when friends burst into the room with the news that the war had ended. . .

Slowing Down Production

Groves wanted me in Washington to discuss the various actions that would be required upon the termination of hostilities. Anticipating the president's announcement, I invited myself to dinner with friends, and a group of us were together when at 7:00 P.M. on August 14, President Truman announced that he had received a message from the Japanese government that he deemed unconditional surrender, a full acceptance of the Potsdam Proclamation. We were all elated by the news. With the official Smyth Report [official government report on the Manhattan Project] released, now there was plenty of leeway for discussion and answering questions about the A-bomb. All my friends had been wondering what I had been doing. But the big news was that the war was over. Wives no longer had to worry about their husbands transferring to the Pacific Theater. We joined the exuberant crowd in the streets of Washington. It was a great evening that lasted into the early-morning hours.

I stayed in Washington until the eighteenth. We knew it would require considerable time for Congress to establish long-range policy. However, plans had to be made for the immediate future. We no longer had the justification of war to warrant an all-out urgent effort; emphasis had to be put on making economies. . .

In December, one reactor was shut down for maintenance, but with the diagnosis of the Wigner disease (the swelling of graphite due to radiation), it was decided to keep one reactor in a standby status and operate only two reactors. We did this to ensure that we would have at least one reactor available for irradiating material for bomb initiators. As a result of these decisions, the production of U-235 actually increased and that of plutonium decreased during 1945 and 1946.

Determining the Effects of the Bomb

Of more immediate concern was determination of the effects of the two atomic bombs at Hiroshima and Nagasaki. Various survey groups were sent to Japan to determine the extent of destruction and the effects of radiation. The radiation survey teams under Staff Warren were organized and left San Francisco on August 14. General Farrell, Warren, and others reached Hiroshima on September 8 and Nagasaki on October 8, and returned to the United States on October 15. Warren reported:

> Japanese physicians and scientists were extremely helpful during the survey, and the general population, including those injured by the bomb, acted as patients act everywhere. There were no incidents, even though the survey party were in the bomb-shattered cities and elsewhere in Japan before the country was occupied by U.S. troops.
>
> It was the consensus of the U.S. survey team and of all the Japanese with whom its members came into contact that a coastal assault on Japan could not have been made without tremendous losses of ships and men, including U.S. casualties of perhaps 500,000, two to four times as many Japanese casualties, and complete destruction of Japan. The use of the atomic bomb, some observers held, gave the Japanese Government the opportunity to surrender without loss of face or need to commit hara-kiri. Fewer were killed by the bomb than had died in the Tokyo-Yokohama raids with conventional bombs. The ethics of the use of the atomic bomb had been raised by U.S. newspapermen in Tokyo, but many Japanese told the survey team they could not understand why the question should have been raised at all: Their own forces would have used it without the slightest qualm if they had had it themselves.
>
> It is realized that this information was not the concern of the survey team, but the discussion came up when fixed coastal gun installations and Kamikaze stations were visited in the downwind area, and it is included for record.

Radioactivity and Blast Damage

In spite of primitive transportation conditions and almost continuous rain, the instruments brought with them by the members of the survey team functioned satisfactorily and lasted well enough to permit an extensive survey of the detonation area in Nagasaki and a somewhat less complete survey of the Hiroshima area, where team activities were hampered by lack of roads in the down (northwest) wind areas.

In all the areas examined, ground contamination with radioactive materials was found to be below the hazardous limit; when the readings were extrapolated back to zero hour, the levels were not considered to be of great significance. The explanation was that the detonation occurred at altitude 1,800 ft., and the fireball therefore did not actually touch the ground. Vaporized materials arose from the ground in the updraft and mixed with fissioned materials, but at that, the amount of radioactive contamination was lower than had been expected.

In Nagasaki, where the affected area was examined more thoroughly than in Hiroshima, the approximate center of the detonation was indicated by a uniform charring of the top and sides of a single fencepost. Other posts in the same area were more charred on one side than on others. Trees, walls, and other standing objects leaned outward spokewise from this central point. The effect was particularly notable to the northeast, up the low hill on which the prison was located.

Induced radioactivity from neutron bombardment could be demonstrated in sulfur insulators, copper wires, and brass objects, in human and animal bones, and in the silver amalgam in human teeth, for a distance of about a thousand meters from the assumed mid point of the destroyed area. The neutron effects ceased rather sharply. It is unfortunate that it was not possible to make precise enough measurements to determine the full extent of the affected area.

The wind at the time of the Nagasaki detonation carried the debris to the east. It could be traced along the roads to the ocean for 90 to 100 miles in a path at least 40 miles wide at the seashore.

Nagasaki lies in the Urakami Valley, which is generally narrow but is about 2,500 meters wide at the detonation point. The eastern wall of the valley rises almost 2,000 feet above the valley floor. The hills were covered by terraces and rocks, and there were almost no dwellings to be damaged. In the next valley, however, the fallout path crossed the north end of the reservoir that supplied the city and also the houses to the north of it. The remainder of the town south of the northern reservoir and some part of the lower Urakami Valley and the harbor area were virtually unaffected by contamination.

Blast effects were well marked for 2,000 meters north and south of the central detonation point in the Urakami Valley. Many peculiar concentration and skip effects were clearly evident, especially in a long series of steel frame buildings of the steel and torpedo works that ran north and south toward the harbor from the central area. Other stronger concrete and steel buildings had suffered obvious structural damage. Most concrete buildings had lost their steel window frames, which, it was evident, could become dangerous missiles inside the buildings.

In the Nagasaki Medical School, bodies were found entangled in the twisted window frames of the laboratory wing, which faced the blast. The contents of many rooms consisted of the wainscoting, the window frames, the ceiling, equipment, linens, and papers, which were all distributed over the floor in a somewhat circular pattern. Many fuses had apparently been replaced with metal coins, and the fixtures hanging from the ceiling had therefore been violently twisted by the blast. The resulting short circuits had apparently lasted long enough to set the ceiling afire in many rooms, with the further result that the contents of the rooms burned along with the bodies of the staff. The prevailing wind carried the fire to the northeast part of the building, along the maple flooring and even up the maple treads of the staircase. The maple-floored ward areas on the upper floors were also burned but only downwind from the staircase.

Many fires apparently occurred from similar short circuits. Overturned stoves caused many others. In both Hiroshima and Nagasaki there was considerable testimony to the effect that the fires started in multiple places at once but did not burn vigorously until about half an hour after the detonation.

The blast wave apparently put out the flames produced by infrared radiation in ripe brown wheat and smoldering wooden and dark surfaces before the fires from this source grew to any size.

Clinical Considerations

When the survey team arrived in both Hiroshima and Nagasaki, it found feeble evidence of first aid efforts. Injured casualties lay wherever any sort of roof offered shelter from the elements. Mats were laid on the floor, and the Prefectorial Government in charge of the country delivered rice and tea to the patients. Helmets had apparently been used for carrying water to them. Later, some of the supposed patients were obviously malingerers, who had come to the aid stations for foods.

From their own observations and from testimony of Japanese, members of the survey team divided the morbidity and mortality of the atomic bombs that were dropped on Japan into the following phases:

1. Very large numbers of persons were crushed in their homes and in the building in which they were working. Their skeletons could be seen in the debris and ashes for almost 1,500 meters from the center of the blast, particularly in the downwind directions. The remains of large numbers of bodies were seen in poorly constructed trench shelters along the main roads. An occasional fresh body, with evidences of purpura, was found in ruined buildings. Collections of shoes (geta) were seen outside many of the first aid stations, where piles of human ashes were left from the extensive cremations carried out in the first few weeks after the bombings; all bodies were cremated, at first, for military reasons, to conceal the number of dead, and later to clean up the area for sanitary reasons. Parties from the Japanese Army and the Prefectorial Government were still searching for bodies as late as 25 September.

2. Large numbers of the population walked for considerable distances after the detonation before they collapsed and died. Many who crowded on the trains that left both cities several hours after the blast died promptly, and their bodies were taken off at the first and second stops.

3. Large numbers developed vomiting and bloody and watery diarrhea (vomitus and bloody feces were found on the floor in many of the aid stations), associated with extreme weakness. They died in the first and second weeks after the bombs were dropped. These manifestations gave rise to fear of typhoid and dysentery, neither of which developed.

4. During this same period deaths from internal injuries and from burns were common. Either the heat from the fires or infrared radiation from the detonations caused many burns, particularly on bare skin or under dark clothing.

5. After a lull without peak mortality from any special causes, death began to occur from purpura, which was often associated with epilation, anemia, and a yellowish coloration of the skin. The so-called bone marrow syndrome, manifested by a low white blood cell count and almost complete absence of the platelets necessary to prevent bleeding, was probably at its maximum between the fourth and sixth weeks after the bombs were dropped (that is, between 10 and 20 September). Most patients with purpura died within a few days after it appeared, but some of them were ob-

Feeling Pride and Shame at Los Alamos

The scientists and technicians at Los Alamos Laboratory had worked extremely hard at developing the atomic bomb for over two and a half years. Their efforts produced spectacular results on August 6, 1945, the day "Little Boy" was dropped on Hiroshima. The reaction at Los Alamos was a mixture of elation and horror. After Hiroshima, the men and women working at Los Alamos began to ask themselves whether they should be proud of their hard work or should they feel ashamed of the destructive force they had unleashed. Or as historian Robert Jungk writes in his book, Brighter than a Thousand Suns, *"was it possible . . . for one and the same person to feel pride and shame simultaneously?"*

The minds of the atomic physicists at Los Alamos had been greatly disturbed and bewildered by the news of the bomb dropped on Hiroshima. O.R. Frisch remembers that one day he suddenly heard loud cries of delight in the corridor outside his study. When he opened the door he saw some of his younger colleagues rushing along with yells of "Whoopee!," like an Indian war cry. They had just heard, over the radio, President Truman reading the report by General Groves of the successful use of the first atom bomb. "It seemed to me that shouts of joy were rather inappropriate," Frisch noted dryly. It was he who, in 1939, had first calculated what enormous energy would be released by splitting the atomic nucleus. That energy had now destroyed tens of thousands of lives.

August 6, 1945, was a black day for people like Einstein, Franck, Szilard and Rabinowitch, who had done their best to prevent use of the bomb. But the men and women up on the mesa were in a quandary. After all, they had worked day and night to achieve their goal. Should they now be proud of what they had done, as it was generally considered they ought to be, in this first moment of surprise? Or should they be ashamed of their work when they thought of the suffering it had caused so many defenseless people? Or again, was it possible—and this position would be the strangest of all, really only comparable with the contradictory data of atomic physics—for one and the same person to feel pride and shame simultaneously? . . .

Robert Brode, one of the American physicists who had studied in Göttingen twenty years before, tried to describe his own feelings and those of some of his companions at Los Alamos at that time in the following terms:

> We were naturally shocked by the effect our weapon had produced, and in particular because the bomb had not been aimed, as we had assumed, specifically at the military establishments in Hiroshima, but dropped in the center of the town. But if I am to tell the whole truth I must confess that our relief was really greater than our horror. For at last our families and friends in other cities and countries knew why we had disappeared for years on end. They had now realized that we, too, had been doing our duty. Finally we ourselves also learned that our work had not been in vain. Speaking for myself, I can say that I had no feelings of guilt.

"Willie" Higinbotham, a thirty-four-year-old electronics specialist—the son of a Protestant clergyman and soon afterward prominent among those atomic scientists who felt politically and morally responsible for their work—wrote from Los Alamos, to his mother:

> I am not a bit proud of the job we have done . . . the only reason for doing it was to beat the rest of the world to a draw . . . perhaps this is so devastating that man will be forced to be peaceful. The alternative to peace is now unthinkable. But unfortunately there will always be some who don't think. . . . I think I now know the meaning of "mixed emotions." I am afraid that Gandhi is the only real disciple of Christ at present . . . anyway it is over for now and God give us strength in the future.

Robert Jungk, *Brighter than a Thousand Suns.* San Diego: Harcourt Brace Jovanovich, Inc., 1958.

served in the aid stations by the survey team. Deaths from purpura occurred a few days earlier and stopped a few days earlier at Hiroshima than at Nagasaki, but otherwise the reactions in both cities were much the same in respect to both clinical manifestations and timing.

Epilation, anemia, and purpura were only occasionally seen in general surviving population, the assumption being that radiation sufficient to cause these pathologic changes was likely to be lethal. Nonetheless, an occasional patient with purpura, particularly if it developed late in September, seemed to have some power of recovery.

6. The death rate after 20 September was much lower than in the preceding weeks, though many casualties continued to die from protracted anemia, secondary infection, burns, and other complications.

As soon as patients with bone marrow and other injuries died in the aid stations, the spaces they had occupied were filled with patients with severe burns who had survived and who were brought in by farmers and others of local population, chiefly to take advantage of the rice and tea available there, as well as of occasional visits by physicians.

7. No count could be made of those who died outside of the devastated area, in public schools or other buildings to which they had been taken for care.

8. Occasional survivors (misses) in the devastated area showed little or no effects of radiation. Some of them had been in deep shelters or inside large buildings, but some escapes could not be explained.

9. The real mortality of the atomic bombs that were dropped on Japan will never be known. The Japanese had no accurate census at the time of the bombing. Afterward, no census was possible. Bodies were hastily cremated, as already mentioned. The destruction and overwhelming chaos made orderly counting impossible. It is not unlikely that the estimates of killed and wounded in Hiroshima (150,000) and Nagasaki (75,000) are overestimated.

Therapy

Occasional attempts to treat casualties showing bone marrow injuries with transfusions, plasma infusions, and penicillin were soon discontinued, chiefly because any needle puncture resulted in serosanguinous oozing that continued to death. Even pricks to obtain blood for blood counts caused oozing that could not be checked. It was thought that if the platelets were not too greatly reduced, because some functioning bone marrow was left, supportive treatment might be useful in carefully selected patients. If laboratory tests showed that the bone marrow was completely destroyed, the treatment available at the time the bombs were dropped on Japan was of no value at all.

Controversy over Radiation

Although the largest number of casualties at Hiroshima and Nagasaki were caused by blast and heat from the explosion and the resulting fires, the effects of radiation have been emphasized as the most horrible and the most feared aspect of atomic war. We were fairly well informed about radiation, but there was plenty that we did not know about it at that time. Our knowledge about the amount and nature of the radiation that would be generated by the bomb was not precise. The Japanese did not know how best to treat those suffering from much larger doses of radiation than man had ever encountered before. We had done extensive research to improve our knowledge, but research data available could not possibly answer all the questions that would be created by the first use of the atomic bomb on a city. We did know that the bomb would generate various types of radiation and neutrons. We had a good idea about what would be a lethal dose, and we knew that there would be many deaths and injuries caused by radiation as well as by heat and blast. We thought correctly that the blast effect of the bomb would be the most effective in causing casualties and destruction, so we tried to maximize that by setting the height of burst at approximately two thousand feet. With this height, we knew there would be radiation and heat casualties. How many we did not know. We also believed that at this height the residual radiation on the ground would be minimized. We wanted little or no residual radiation because we hoped that our troops would soon occupy the city, and we did not want to endanger them.

The number of casualties to be caused by radiation was considered but was not a major factor of the decision to use or not to use the atomic bomb. However, the number of radiation casualties, the general effects of radiation, the action of radiation on living tissues, the genetic effects, and the number of cases of cancer among the survivors have been matters of controversy for over forty years. To get some of the answers, both Warren and [Dr. Robert S.] Stone advocated more research. The Atomic Bomb Casualty Commission and its successor, the Radiation Effects Research Foundation, have conducted studies and have found an excess of about 250 cancer fatalities attributable to radiation exposure over the years 1950–78. This excess can be compared with about forty-eight hundred normal cancer deaths, and 23,500 deaths from all causes for the A-bomb survivors under study for the same period. This excess number may increase with time, and the study continues. But the number is relatively small compared to some of the exaggerated claims. The studies also have failed to find any statistically significant increase of genetic effects. Likewise, there have been no irreversible environmental effects, and as anticipated, there was little dangerous residual radiation in Hiroshima or Nagasaki.

Recently I heard of new findings concerning the relative hazards of neutrons as compared to ionizing radiation. However, my informant hastened to add that this new finding does not have any material effect on the overall casualties. We are still learning. Such controversies and new findings will continue, but they do not materially change the horrible effect of nuclear or thermonuclear war.

The most important military effect was that it required only two atomic bombs to end the war. The planned invasion of Japan was not necessary. The two bombs probably saved many tens of thousands of lives, and ending the war certainly justified the decision to use them. It also made the world aware of atomic weapons. The initial public reaction undoubtedly exaggerated the effect of an atomic bomb. The shock effect and the fact that Japan was already defeated destroyed their will to fight. I have always believed that if the bomb had not been used, any demonstration or test probably would have been underrated and, as a result, atomic weapons might not have been as effective as deterrents for avoiding war between the United States and the Soviet Union. Moreover, not using the A-bomb would not have avoided the race for nuclear supremacy between the United States and the USSR. Although we did not know it for sure at the time, the USSR was already working on their own A-bomb before the war ended.

Proposing an Atomic Energy Agency

Dwight D. Eisenhower

President Dwight D. Eisenhower delivered this "Atoms for Peace" speech to the General Assembly of the United Nations in 1953. At that time, atomic bombs were twenty-five times more powerful than the ones dropped on Japan, and the United States was no longer the sole nuclear power. The Soviet Union had also developed nuclear arms, and Eisenhower predicted that in the future all nations may possess nuclear weapons. As he spoke to the United Nations, the possibility of a nuclear war loomed over the world as the United States and Russia squared off in the tense Cold War era. A nuclear exchange between the United States and Russia could mean the destruction of civilization and even the eradication of the human race.

Eisenhower proposed talks with the Soviet Union to limit and control nuclear weapons. He further proposed to transform nuclear energy from a destructive weapon into an instrument for prosperity and peace. To accomplish this goal, an international Atomic Energy Agency would be established under the authority of the United Nations. This agency would be responsible for collecting fissionable materials and providing secure facilities where the radioactive fuel would be "immune to surprise seizure." World scientists working for the Atomic Energy Agency would apply the new energy source to "the needs of agriculture, medicine, and other peaceful activities," as well as to generating electrical energy in "the power starved areas of the world." Thus, as Eisenhower hoped, through international regulation, the dark

Excerpted from Dwight D. Eisenhower's address to the United Nations General Assembly, December 8, 1953.

shadow of atomic power would bring about hope and prosperity for all nations. The International Atomic Energy Agency (IAEA) was established as an autonomous organization under the United Nations in 1957. From its headquarters located in Vienna, Austria, the agency continues to assist and monitor its 133 member states to this day.

M adame President [Vijaya Pandit], Members of the General Assembly:

When [U.N.] Secretary General Dag Hammarskjold's invitation to address this General Assembly reached me in Bermuda, I was just beginning a series of conferences with the Prime Ministers and Foreign Ministers of Great Britain and of France. Our subject was some of the problems that beset the world.

During the remainder of the Bermuda Conference, I had constantly in mind that ahead of me lay a great honor. That honor is mine today as I stand here, privileged to address the General Assembly of the United Nations.

At the same time that I appreciate the distinction of addressing you, I have a sense of exhilaration as I look upon this assembly.

Never before in history has so much hope for so many people been gathered together in a single organization. Your deliberations and decisions during these somber years have already realized part of those hopes.

But the great tests and the great accomplishments still lie ahead. And in the confident expectation of those accomplishments, I would use the office which, for the time being, I hold, to assure you that the Government of the United States will remain steadfast in its support of this body. This we shall do in the conviction that you will provide a great share of the wisdom, of the courage and the faith which can bring to this world lasting peace for all nations and happiness and well-being for all men. . .

I know that the American people share my deep belief that if a danger exists in the world, it is a danger shared by all—and equally, that if hope exists in the mind of one nation, that hope should be shared by all.

Finally, if there is to be advanced any proposal designed to ease, even by the smallest measure, the tensions of today's world, what more appropriate audience could there be than the members of the General Assembly of the United Nations?

I feel impelled to speak today in a language that, in a sense, is new—one, which I, who spent so much of my life in the military profession, would have preferred never to use.

That new language is the language of atomic warfare.

The atomic age has moved forward at such a pace that every citizen of the world should have some comprehension, at least in comparative terms, of the extent of this development, of the utmost significance to every one of us. Clearly, if the people of the world are to conduct an intelligent search for peace, they must be armed with the significant facts of today's existence.

My recital of atomic danger and power is necessarily stated in United States terms, for these are the only incontrovertible facts that I know. I need hardly point out to this assembly, however, that this subject is global, not merely national in character.

On July 16, 1945, the United States set off the world's first atomic test explosion. Since that date in 1945, the United States of America has conducted forty-two test explosions.

Atomic bombs today are more than twenty-five times as powerful as the weapons with which the atomic age dawned, while hydrogen weapons are in the ranges of millions of tons of TNT equivalent.

Today, the United States' stockpile of atomic weapons, which, of course, increases daily, exceeds by many times the explosive equivalent of the total of all bombs and all shells that came from every plane and every gun in every theatre of war through all the years of World War II.

A single air group, whether afloat or land based, can now deliver to any reachable target a destructive cargo exceeding in power all the bombs that fell on Britain in all of World War II.

In size and variety the development of atomic weapons has been no less remarkable. This development has been such that atomic weapons have virtually achieved conventional status within our armed services. In the United States services, the Army, the Navy, the Air Force and the Marine Corps are all capable of putting this weapon to military use.

But the dread secret and the fearful engines of atomic might are not ours alone.

In the first place, the secret is possessed by our friends and Allies, Great Britain and Canada, whose scientific genius made a tremendous contribution to our original discoveries and the designs of atomic bombs.

The secret is also known by the Soviet Union.

The Soviet Union has informed us that, over recent years, it has devoted extensive resources to atomic weapons. During this period, the Soviet Union has exploded a series of atomic devices, including at least one involving thermonuclear reactions.

If at one time the United States possessed what might have been called a monopoly of atomic power, that monopoly ceased to exist several years ago. Therefore, although our earlier start has permitted us to accumulate what is today a great quantitative advantage, the atomic realities of today comprehend two facts of even greater significance.

First, the knowledge now possessed by several nations will eventually be shared by others, possibly all others.

Second, even a vast superiority in numbers of weapons, and a consequent capability of devastating retaliation, is no preventive, of itself, against the fearful material damage and toll of human lives that would be inflicted by surprise aggression.

The free world, at least dimly aware of these facts, has naturally embarked on a large program of warning and defense systems. That program will be accelerated and expanded.

But let no one think that the expenditure of vast sums for weapons and systems of defense can guarantee absolute safety for the cities and the citizens of any nation. The awful arithmetic of the atomic bomb does not permit of such an easy solution. Even against the most powerful defense, an aggressor in possession of the effective minimum number of atomic bombs or a surprise attack could probably place a sufficient number of his bombs on the chosen targets to cause hideous damage.

Should such an atomic attack be launched against the United States, our reaction would be swift and resolute. But for me to say that the defense capabilities of the United States are such that they could inflict terrible losses upon an aggressor—for me to say that the retaliation capabilities of the United States are so great that such an aggressor's land would be laid waste—all this, while fact, is not the true expression of the purpose and the hope of the United States.

To pause there would be to confirm the hopeless finality of a belief that two atomic colossi are doomed malevolently to eye each other indefinitely across a trembling world. To stop there would be to accept helplessly the probability of civilization destroyed—the annihilation of the irreplaceable heritage of mankind handed down to us generation from generation—and the condemnation of mankind to begin all over again the age-old struggle upward from savagery toward decency and right and justice.

Surely no sane member of the human race could discover victory in such desolation. Could anyone wish his name to be coupled by history with such human degradation and destruction?

Occasional pages of history do record the faces of the "Great Destroyers" but the whole book of history reveals mankind's never-ending quest for peace and mankind's God-given capacity to build.

It is with the book of history, and not with isolated pages, that the United States will ever wish to be identified. My country wants to be constructive, not destructive. It wants agreements, not wars, among nations. It wants, itself, to live in freedom and in the confidence that the people of every other nation enjoy equally the right of choosing their own way of life.

So my country's purpose is to help us move out of the dark chamber of horrors into the light, to find a way by which the minds of men, the hopes of men, the souls of men everywhere, can move forward toward peace and happiness and well-being.

In this quest, I know that we must not lack patience.

I know that in a world divided, such as ours today, salvation cannot be attained by one dramatic act.

I know that many steps will have to be taken over many months before the world can look at itself one day and truly realize that a new climate of mutually peaceful confidence is abroad in the world.

But I know, above all else, that we must start to take these steps—now.

The United States and its Allies, Great Britain and France, have, over the past months, tried to take some of these steps. Let no one say that we shun the conference table. . .

As you already know from our joint Bermuda communique, the United States, Great Britain and France have agreed promptly to meet with the Soviet Union.

The Government of the United States approaches this conference with hopeful sincerity. We will bend every effort of our minds to the single purpose of emerging from that conference with tangible results toward peace—the only true way of lessening international tension.

We never have, we never will, propose to suggest that the Soviet Union surrender what is rightfully theirs.

We will never say that the peoples of Russia are an enemy with whom we have no desire ever to deal or mingle in friendly and fruitful relationship.

On the contrary, we hope that this coming conference may initiate a relationship with the Soviet Union which will eventually bring about a free intermingling of the peoples of the East and of the West—the one sure, human way of developing the understanding required for confident and peaceful relations. . . .

But I do not wish to rest either upon the reiteration of past proposals or the restatement of past deeds. The gravity of the time is such that every new avenue of peace, no matter how dimly discernible, should be explored.

There is at least one new avenue of peace which has not yet been well explored—an avenue now laid out by the General Assembly of the United Nations.

In its resolution of November 18, 1953, this General Assembly suggested—and I quote—"that the Disarmament Commission study the desirability of establishing a sub-committee consisting of representatives of the powers principally involved, which should seek, in private, an acceptable solution—and report such a solution to the General Assembly and to the Security Council not later than 1 September, 1954."

The United States, heeding the suggestion of the General Assembly of the United Nations, is instantly prepared to meet privately with such other countries as may be "principally involved," to seek "an acceptable solution" to the atomic armaments race which overshadows not only the peace but the very life of the world.

We shall carry into these private or diplomatic talks a new conception.

The United States would seek more than the mere reduction or elimination of atomic materials for military purposes.

It is not enough to take this weapon out of the hands of the soldiers. It must be put into the hands of those who will know how to strip its military casing and adapt it to the arts of peace.

The United States knows that if the fearful trend of atomic military build-up can be reversed, this greatest of destructive forces can be developed into a great boon for the benefit of all mankind.

The United States knows that peaceful power from atomic energy is no dream of the future. That capability, already proved, is here now—today. Who can doubt, if the entire body of the world's scientists and engineers had adequate amounts of fissionable material with which to test and develop their ideas, that this capability would rapidly be transformed into universal, efficient and economic usage.

To hasten the day when fear of the atom will begin to disappear from the minds of people and the governments of the

East and West there are certain steps that can be taken now.

I therefore make the following proposals:

The governments principally involved to the extent permitted by elementary prudence, to begin now and continue to make joint contributions from their stockpiles of normal uranium and fissionable materials to an international atomic energy agency. We would expect that such an agency would be set up under the aegis of the United Nations.

The ratios of contributions, the procedures and other details would properly be within the scope of the "private conversations" I have referred to earlier.

The United States is prepared to undertake these explorations in good faith. Any partner of the United States acting in the same good faith will find the United States a not unreasonable or ungenerous associate.

Undoubtedly initial and early contributions to this plan would be small in quantity. However, the proposal has the great virtue that it can be undertaken without irritations and mutual suspicions incident to any attempt to set up a completely acceptable system of world-wide inspection and control.

The atomic energy agency could be made responsible for the impounding, storage and protection of the contributed fissionable and other material. The ingenuity of our scientists will provide special, safe conditions under which such a bank of fissionable material can be made essentially immune to surprise seizure.

The more important responsibility of this atomic energy agency would be to devise methods whereby this fissionable material would be allocated to serve the peaceful pursuits of mankind. Experts would be mobilized to apply atomic energy to the needs of agriculture, medicine and other peaceful activities. A special purpose would be to provide abundant electrical energy in the power-starved areas of the world. Thus the contributing powers would be dedicating some of their strength to serve the needs rather than the fears of mankind.

The United States would be more than willing—it would

be proud—to take up with others "principally involved" the development of plans whereby such peaceful use of atomic energy would be expedited.

Of those "principally involved" the Soviet Union must, of course, be one.

I would be prepared to submit to the Congress of the United States, and with every expectation of approval, any such plan that would:

First, encourage world-wide investigation into the most effective peacetime uses of fissionable material;

Second, begin to diminish the potential destructive power of the world's atomic stockpiles;

Third, allow all peoples of all nations to see that, in this enlightened age, the great powers of the earth, both of the East and of the West, are interested in human aspirations first rather than building up the armaments of war;

Fourth, open up a new channel for peaceful discussion and initiate at least a new approach to the many difficult problems that must be solved in both private and public conversations if the world is to shake off the inertia imposed by fear and is to make positive progress toward peace.

Against the dark background of the atomic bomb, the United States does not wish merely to present strength, but also the desire and the hope for peace.

The coming months will be fraught and fateful decisions. In this Assembly, in the capitals and military headquarters of the world; in the hearts of men everywhere, be they governed or governors, may they be the decisions which will lead this world out of fear and into peace.

To the making of these fateful decisions, the United States pledges before you—and therefore before the world—its determination to help solve the fearful atomic dilemma—to devote its entire heart and mind to find the way by which the miraculous inventiveness of man shall not be dedicated to his death, but consecrated to his life.

I again thank the delegates for the great honor they have done me in inviting me to appear before them and in listening to me so courteously. Thank you.

The Need for a National Nuclear Energy Program

the Atomic Energy Commission

The Atomic Energy Commission (AEC) was established by Congress in 1946 to regulate the production of atomic power. It was the civilian successor to the military's Manhattan Project that developed the atomic bomb. The commission's main tasks were the production of fissionable materials, safety, and the production of electric power. Its most important function, however, was to put the great promise and power of nuclear energy into the hands of civilians and private industry.

In this 1962 report submitted to President John F. Kennedy, the AEC argued that because America is a technological society, it needs abundant sources of energy. The report predicted that the supply of fossil fuels—oil and gas—would be exhausted some time in the twenty-first century. Accordingly, for the United States to prosper, it must find new sources of energy. Uranium and nuclear energy have the potential to supply the nation with "unlimited amounts of latent energy." The report advocates a strong national program to foster nuclear power to generate electricity for America's energy needs.

The AEC projected that efficient nuclear reactors would be economically attractive by the 1980s with half the nation's energy produced by nuclear generation by the end of the 1990s. The report further predicted billions of dollars saved through more efficient energy production as well as increased

Excerpted from *Civilian Nuclear Power: A Report to the President—1962*, by the U.S. Atomic Energy Commission (Washington, DC: U.S. Government Printing Office, 1962). Reprinted with permission.

prosperity from the abundance of nuclear energy. To put a national nuclear energy program into effect, the AEC proposed to fund research on improving reactor design as well as the construction of new nuclear power plants. These steps would promote and maintain the United States' technological leadership in the field of nuclear power and solve its energy needs both short-term and in the future. The AEC would transform into the U.S. Department of Energy in 1977.

Our technological society requires ample sources of energy. Although large, the supplies of fossil fuels are not unlimited and, furthermore, these materials are especially valuable for many specific purposes as transportation, small isolated heat and power installations, and as sources of industrial chemicals. Reasonable amounts should be preserved for future generations.

Comparison of estimates of fossil fuel resources with projections of the rapidly increasing rate of energy consumption predicts that, if no additional forms of energy were utilized, we would exhaust our readily available, low cost fossil fuels in a century or less and our presently visualized total supplies in about another century. In actual fact, long before they become exhausted we will be obliged to taper off their rate of use by supplementing them increasingly from other sources.

In contrast, our supplies of uranium and thorium contain almost unlimited amounts of latent energy that can be tapped provided "breeder" reactors are developed to convert the fertile materials, uranium-238 and thorium-232, to fissionable plutonium-239 and uranium-233, respectively. Successfully done, this will render relatively unimportant the cost of nuclear raw materials so that even very low-grade sources will become economically acceptable.

The use of nuclear energy for electric power and, less immediately, for industrial process heat and other purposes is technically feasible and economically reasonable. In addition to its ultimate importance as a means of exploiting a large new energy resource, nuclear electric power holds important near-term possibilities: as a means of significantly reducing power generation costs, especially in areas where fossil fuel costs are high; as an important contributor to new industrial technology and to our technological world leadership; as a significant positive element in our foreign trade; and, potentially, as a means of strengthening our national defense.

In view of the above we have concluded that: Nuclear energy can and should make an important and, ultimately, a vital contribution toward meeting our long-term energy requirements, and, in particular, that: the development and exploitation of nuclear electric power is clearly in the near- and long-term national interest and should be vigorously pursued.

The Role of the Federal Government

The technological development of nuclear power is expensive. The reactors are complex, and operating units, even of a scaled-down test variety, must of necessity be large and costly. Furthermore, nuclear power does not meet a hitherto unfilled need but must depend for marketability on purely economic advantages that will return the development investment slowly. Hence, the equipment industry could not have afforded to undertake the program by itself. The Government must clearly play a role.

An early objective should be to reach the point where, with appropriate encouragement and support, industry can provide nuclear power installations of economic attractiveness sufficient to induce utilities to install them at their own expense. Once this is achieved the Government should devote itself to advanced developments designed to meet long-range objectives, leaving to industry responsibility for nearer-term improvements. Gradually, as technological maturity is reached, the transition to industry should become complete.

Thus, the proper role of Government is to take the lead in developing and demonstrating the technology in such ways that economic factors will promote industrial applications in the public interest and lead to a self-sustaining and growing nuclear power industry.

Reactors for Electric Power

Accordingly, in keeping with national policy, and with the [role] assigned to it by the Atomic Energy Act, the Atomic Energy Commission has conducted and encouraged a vigorous program directed toward the development and extensive exploitation of nuclear energy for civilian purposes, with emphasis on nuclear electric power. About $1.275 billion has been expended by the AEC to date on the civilian power program. This program has included both research and development and a "power demonstration" program, involving aid in the construction and operation of practical reactors on utility grids. Several reactor types are under development. Most highly developed are "converter" reactors that produce less fissionable material than they consume; much less far along are "breeder" reactors that produce more than they consume.

In one segment of the power demonstration program, Commission-built and -owned "prototype" reactors are operated by utilities that buy the steam; in another segment, utilities are given research and development assistance in designing and constructing their own reactors and, for a few years no charge is made for the lease of Government-owned nuclear fuel. Six sizeable reactors of the more highly developed types are in successful operation on utility grids (the two largest without AEC assistance); seven more will be completed by the end of 1963; a few others are under construction or nearly so. Experience has shown that nuclear electric power is readily achieved technically but difficulties have been met in developing a technology that is economically competitive with conventional power generation methods. Happily, in recent years these difficulties have been progressively overcome.

Certain classes of power reactors, notably water-cooled converters producing saturated steam are now on the threshold of economic competitiveness with conventional power in large installations in high fossil fuel cost areas of the country. Foreseeable improvements will substantially increase the areas of competitiveness. . . .

In our opinion, economic nuclear power is so near at hand that only a modest additional incentive is required to initiate its appreciable early use by the utilities. Should this occur the normal economic processes would, we feel, result in expansion at a rapid rate. The Government's investment would be augmented many fold by industry. Equipment manufacturers could finance major technical developments, thus reducing the future need for Government participation.

Continuation of the Commission's present effort, with some augmentation in support for the power demonstration program, and with program adjustments to give added emphasis to breeders, would, we believe, provide industry with the needed stimulus to build a significant number of large reactors in the near future, would bring nuclear power to a competitive status with conventional power throughout most of the country during the 1970's, and would make breeder reactors economically attractive by the 1980's.

Advantages of Nuclear Power

Under these conditions, we estimate that by the end of the century nuclear power would be assuming the total increase in national electric energy requirements and would be providing half the energy generated. This rate of progress, projected into the next century, would be an important step in conservation of the fossil fuels and, unless breeders lagged the converters much more than we predict, would raise no problems in nuclear fuel supplies.

Under conservative cost assumptions, it is estimated that by the end of the century the above projected use of nuclear power would result in cumulative savings in generation costs of about $30 billion. The annual saving would be between $4 and $5 billion. High cost power areas would no longer exist, since, in the absence of significant fuel transportation expenses, the cost of nuclear power is essentially the same everywhere. This would be an economic boon to areas of high cost fossil fuels and, by enabling them to compete better, should increase the industrial potential of the entire country.

More generally, the introduction of nuclear power technology on a significant scale would add to the health and vigor of our industry and general economy. Technical progress would assist the space and military programs and have other ancillary benefits. Our international leadership in the field would be maintained, with benefit to our prestige and our foreign trade. Nuclear power could also improve our defense posture; it would not burden the transportation system during national emergencies; furthermore, the "containment" required for safety reasons could, if desired, be achieved at little, if any, extra cost by underground installations, thus "hardening" the plants against nuclear attack.

A substantially lesser program would sharply reduce these benefits. Too great a slowdown could result in losing significant portions of industry's present nuclear capability thereby seriously delaying the time at which it would assume a major share of the development costs.

On the other hand we do not believe that a major step-up in the whole Commission program is appropriate. Taken as a whole, support of the scientists and engineers engaged in developmental work is about adequate and, in view of the country's other needs, it would seem unwarranted to increase appreciably such manpower in this field.

To summarize we have concluded that the nuclear power program should continue on an expeditious basis. Commission support should continue with added emphasis on stimulating industrial participation. The program should include: (1) early construction of plants of the presently most competitive reactor types; (2) development, construction and demonstration of advanced converters to improve the economics and the use of nuclear fuels; (3) intensive development and, later, demonstration of breeder reactors to fill the long-range needs of utilizing fertile as well as fissile fuels.

An important corollary area is the development of economical chemical reprocessing methods whereby useful fissile and fertile materials are recaptured from used fuel assemblies and the fission products are removed. Another important line of work concerns the ultimate storage or disposal of the large amounts of radioactive fission products that will be generated when a major power industry comes into being.

An overriding consideration is that of safety. Not only must inherent safety be assured in fact but its existence must be conclusively demonstrated to the public. With adequate technical improvements and the accumulation of satisfactory experience, it should be possible gradually to remove many of the siting restrictions in force today, thus permitting plant locations closer to the large load centers.

Possible Construction Program

A composite construction program for the next dozen years might entail the following: (1) the construction and placing into operation of seven or eight power-producing prototype reactors, approximately half of which would be advanced converters and the rest breeders; most of their cost would probably be borne by the AEC; (2) assistance, as necessary, to industry in the construction of 10–12 full-scale power plants of improving design as time goes on; hopefully, industry will concurrently bear full costs of many more of well proven design.

This construction would, of course, be backed by specific development programs directed at the more advanced reactor types, especially breeders, and by research and development related to the underlying technology. . . .

Objectives for the Future

Clearly: The overall objective of the Commission's nuclear power program should be to foster and support the growing use of nuclear energy and, importantly, to guide the program in such directions as to make possible the exploitation of the vast energy resources latent in the fertile materials, uranium-238 and thorium. More specific objectives may be summarized as follows:

1. The demonstration of economic nuclear power by assuring the construction of plants incorporating the presently most competitive reactor types;

2. The early establishment of a self-sufficient and growing nuclear power industry that will assume an increasing share of the development costs;

3. The development of improved converter and, later, breeder reactors to convert the fertile isotopes to fissionable ones, thus making available the full potential of the nuclear fuels.

4. The maintenance of U.S. technological leadership in the world by means of a vigorous domestic nuclear power program and appropriate cooperation with, and assistance to, our friends abroad.

The role of the Commission in achieving these objectives must be one of positive and vigorous leadership, both to achieve the technical goals and to assure growing participation by the equipment and utility industry as nuclear power becomes economic in increasing areas of this country and the world at large.

Chronology

1903

The husband and wife team of Marie and Pierre Curie received the Nobel Prize in physics for their discovery of radium.

1911

Ernest Rutherford advances the planetary model of the atom.

1932

James Chadwick discovers the neutron.

1933

January 30: Adolf Hitler becomes chancellor of Germany.

Spring–Summer: Physicists James Franck, Edward Teller, Leo Szilard, Eugene Wigner, and Albert Einstein are persecuted by the Nazis for being Jewish and flee Germany for the United States.

1934

Enrico Fermi bombards uranium with neutrons and publishes his experimental results.

1938

November: Italian born Fermi receives Nobel Prize for physics in Sweden, and then emigrates to the United States to escape Itlian dictator Benito Mussolini's anti-Semitic policies.

December: Otto Hahn and Fritz Strassmann, two German physicists, split uranium atom, creating lighter elements, energy, and more neutrons. Their discoveries would be the basis for devising the atomic bomb.

1939
January: Otto Frisch and Lise Meitner prove a "fission" reaction occurred in Hahn and Strassman's experiment.

August 2: Albert Einstein signs letter to President Roosevelt warning that atomic bomb is possible.

September 1: Germany invades Poland. World War II begins.

October: The Uranium Committee was formed to advise Roosevelt on development of an atomic bomb.

1940
Leo Szilard and Enrico Fermi begin studies for the U.S. government on building an atomic pile.

1941
February: Glenn T. Seaborg and Emilio Segrè discover plutonium, the fuel for the "Fat Man" atomic bomb.

July: Britain's MAUD Committee reports that the atomic bomb could be built before the end of the war.

December 7: Japan attacks the U.S. naval base at Pearl Harbor, Hawaii.

December 8: United States declares war on Japan.

December 11: Germany and Italy declare war on the United States.

Roosevelt commits the United States to produce atomic weapons.

1942
September 17: Brigadier General Leslie Groves becomes the military head of the Manhattan Project, the organization created to build the atomic bomb for the United States.

October: Groves selects J. Robert Oppenheimer as scientific director of the Manhattan Project.

December 2: The first atomic pile, under the direction of Enrico Fermi, sustains a controlled nuclear chain reaction at the Metallurgical Laboratory at the University of Chicago.

December 7: Los Alamos Ranch School in New Mexico is chosen for the site of the Los Alamos Laboratory. It will centralize and direct the design of the atomic bomb for the Manhattan Project.

1944

November 7: Franklin D. Roosevelt is re-elected president for fourth term with Harry S. Truman as his vice president.

December: Physicist Klaus Fuchs arrives at Los Alamos among a group of scientists from Britain.

1945

February: Fuchs first passes atomic bomb secrets to the Soviet Union.

Spring: American bombers drop incendiary bombs on Tokyo, Yokohama, and other Japanese cities.

April 12: Roosevelt dies in office and Truman becomes president.

April 25: Truman is informed of the Manhattan Project and its secret mission to develop the atomic bomb.

May 7: Germany surrenders.

June 12: The Franck Report, written by seven Manhattan Project scientists, is given to Secretary of War Stimson. The report advises against dropping the atom bomb on Japan and instead suggests a warning demonstration.

July 15: The first atomic test explosion, known as the Trinity Test, takes place at Alamogordo, New Mexico.

July 17: Leo Szilard sends petition signed by over sixty scientists calling on the president not to use the bomb against Japan.

July 27: The United States, Britain, and China issue the Potsdam Declaration calling for Japan to surrender.

August 6: The first atomic bomb, "Little Boy," is dropped on Hiroshima.

August 8: The Soviet Union declares war on Japan.

August 9: The United States drops the second atomic bomb, "Fat Man," on Nagasaki.

August 14: Japan officially accepts the Allied conditions for surrender.

1946
The Baruch Plan to eliminate nuclear weapons and put atomic energy under international controls is presented to the United Nations.

1947
January 1: The Atomic Energy Commission is created by Congress. The AEC establishes civilian authority over atomic energy and nuclear weapons.

Spring: The first Russian atomic pile sustains a chain reaction.

1949
The Soviets conduct their first atomic bomb test explosion.

1950
January: Klaus Fuchs is arrested in Britain for passing atomic bomb secrets to the Soviet Union.

Truman decides to go ahead on studies for the hydrogen bomb.

1951
Experimental production of electricity from nuclear power begins.

1952
November 1: The United States conducts the hydrogen bomb test at Eniwetok atoll in the Marshall Islands.

1953
December: President Eisenhower gives "Atoms for Peace" speech before the United Nations proposing international controls on atomic energy and nuclear weapons.

1955
The Soviet Union explodes a hydrogen bomb.

1957
The first commercial nuclear power plant begins operation.

1972
The Strategic Arms Limitations Talks (SALT) between the United States and USSR produces Anti-Ballistic Missile Treaty. These talks begin the gradual reduction of nuclear weapons in the two nuclear superpowers' arsenals.

For Further Research

Hans A. Bethe, *The Road from Los Alamos.* New York: Simon and Schuster, 1991.

Don E. Beyer, *The Manhattan Project.* New York: Franklin Watts, 1991.

Michael Blow, *The History of the Atomic Bomb.* New York: Harper and Row, 1968.

Arthur Holly Compton, *Atomic Quest: A Personal Narrative.* New York: Oxford University Press, 1956.

Laura Fermi, *Atoms in the Family.* Chicago: University of Chicago, 1954.

Otto Frisch, *What Little I Remember.* New York: Cambridge University Press, 1979.

Samuel Glasstone and Philip T. Colan, *The Effects of Nuclear Weapons.* Washington, DC: Government Printing Office, 1977.

Doreen Gonzales, *The Manhattan Project and the Atomic Bomb in American History.* Berkeley Heights, NJ: Enslow Publishers, 2000.

Leslie Groves, *Now It Can Be Told.* New York: Harper and Row, Publishers, 1962.

John Hersey, *Hiroshima.* New York: Alfred A. Knopf, 1946.

Robert Jungk, *Brighter than a Thousand Suns.* New York: Harcourt Brace Janovich, 1958.

James W. Kunetka, *City of Fire: Los Alamos and the Birth of the Atomic Age, 1943–1945.* Englewood Cliffs, NJ: Prentice-Hall, 1978.

William D. Leahy, *I Was There.* New York: Arno Press, 1979.

Richard S. Lewis and Jane Wilson, eds., *Alamogordo Plus Twenty-Five.* New York: Viking Press, 1970.

Leona Marshall Libby, *The Uranium People.* New York: Charles Scribner's Sons, 1979.

K.D. Nichols, *The Road to Trinity.* New York: William Morrow, 1987.

Richard Rhodes, *The Making of the Atomic Bomb.* New York: Simon and Schuster, 1986.

Tamara L. Roleff, ed., *The Atom Bomb.* San Diego: Greenhaven Press, 2000.

Kyoko Seldon and Mark Seldon, eds., *The Atomic Bomb: Voices from Hiroshima and Nagasaki.* Armonk, NY: M.E. Sharpe, 1989.

Henry D. Smyth, *Atomic Energy for Military Purposes.* Princeton: Princeton University Press, 1947.

Henry L. Stimson, *On Active Service in Peace and War.* New York: Harper & Brothers, 1947.

Ferenc Morton Szasz, *The Day the Sun Rose Twice.* Albuquerque: University of New Mexico Press, 1984.

Edward Teller, *Memoirs: A Twentieth-Century Journey in Science and Politics.* Cambridge, MA: Perseus Publishing, 2001.

Paul W. Tibbets Jr., *The Tibbets Story.* New York: Stein and Day, 1978.

Harry S. Truman, *Memoirs. Volume One: Year of Decisions.* Garden City, NY: Doubleday, 1955.

Stafford L. Warren, *The Role of Radiology in the Development of the Atomic Bomb.* Washington, DC: Surgeon General's Office, 1966.

Spencer R. Weart and Gertrude Weiss Szilard, eds., *Leo Szilard: His Version of the Facts.* Cambridge, MA: MIT Press, 1978.

Robert C. Williams and Philip L. Cantelon, eds., *The American Atom*. Philadelphia: University of Pennsylvania Press, 1984.

Herbert York, *The Advisors: Oppenheimer, Teller, and the Superbomb*. San Francisco, W.H. Freeman, 1976.

Louie B. Young, *The Mystery of Matter*. New York: Oxford University Press, 1965.

Index

G4/YA

BOSTON PUBLIC LIBRARY

3 9999 04455 699 9